ANCHOR OF MY DREAMS

DEDICATED

To

My Family.

My Grandmother

ANCHOR OF MY DREAMS

HANNAH DORIS
WILLIAMS

new horizon

ISBN 0 86116 543 8

Published and Printed by
NEW HORIZON (Transeuros Limited)
BOGNOR REGIS
SUSSEX

ANCHOR OF MY DREAMS

CHAPTER ONE

'The kindly rough feel of Grandma's flannel-
aproned lap under my tender baby-legs,
was LOVE.'

I want to write about my grandmother Rachel Daniel, born Rachel Pryce. I was first really aware of her when, on ironing day, my mother pressed the starched white lace, a few inches wide. I watched it snaking off the kitchen-table on to the flagstone floor, it seemed for miles.

"Sit still, Hannah fach," she said as she lifted me in her warm arms to sit on a chair near the fire in that cosiest of kitchens, which was humid with the hot, clean smell of freshly-washed linen.

On the table stood a bowl of cold water into which she frequently dipped her hand to sprinkle some on clothes that had become too dry and would still be creased if ironed as they were. Thump, thump went the iron as she felt it cooling and another hot one was needed from the roaring fire.

Later, she reeved the couple of yards of lace and sewed it onto a saucer-sized piece of stiff material. Starting at the centre, the lace was sewn round and round to form a large rosette. Black velvet was used to cover the wire round the hem and here was a fresh day-time cap for Grandma.

There were several such caps. My Grandmother unpicked them for washing and my mother transformed them into crowns for her straight, drawn-back grey hair. Grandma came downstairs every morning wearing her cap and wore it all day until we had climbed upstairs to the bedroom where I slept with her, sunk in the lovely, floppy feather-bed on the big brass bedstead.

The making of these caps involved me, to my delight.

"Go up to Miss Thomas's for a yard of 'morve' satin baby-ribbon, there's a good little girl," said my mother, "and if she hasn't got any 'morve' black will do."

Eagerly I took the pennies from her hand, as she added, "If she's out of satin, velvet will be all right."

This ribbon was for making the little bows or bunches that she placed to nestle among the folds of lace, like flowers peeping out of snow.

We lived, my parents, my sister Evelyn, five years my senior, my brother Dick, two years younger than me, several cousins and I, with my grandmother in The Station Inn, Landore, on the outskirts of Swansea. It stood in a terrace of small houses facing a high bank on which the railway lines ran. Visitors who slept in the front bedroom had to be careful to draw their curtains when undressing, as passengers in the Fishguard-London express could see them, at eye-level.

Some trains stopped at Landore for perhaps ten minutes, allowing time for a quick sprint down the steps to the road and up to The Station Inn for a hurried drink.

Nights were noisy with shunting which disturbed friends staying with us, but to us it was a lullaby I missed when I spent my holidays at my Pryce relations' homes in the country. The scent of hay was unfamiliar after the smoke of Landore.

The arrival of a parcel was something important to watch.

"Careful now, Hannah fach," Grandma said, "don't tear the paper if it's nice and stiff, and mind to roll up the cord and put it in Buller." The square tin on the dresser, where cord was kept, showed the face of a fierce soldier, General Buller.

My face fell when I saw how stiff the paper was, but Grandma was pleased. Folding it into strips, eight inches long and two wide, she said sharply, "Come on now, fetch me a knife," and soon there was a neat pile of the strong brown paper strips, the weapons with which she attacked my hair every evening.

"Now, under the cushion on the 'sciw' (settle) with them before your father snatches them for the beer-bungs in the cellar."

How I wished he had seen the parcel first, as he often did, but somehow Grandma never ran out of paper for my hair.

After clearing the table of everything except the hated paper-curlers and a basin of cold water, she said cheerfully, "Now then, move up, merch i" (my girl) and she dipped a large comb into the water, dragged it through my long, fair hair and divided it into eight tresses. I waited for the agony. It wasn't so bad when she started the tight winding of hair round the paper but when the scalp was reached, I screamed "It hurts!"

"Stop grumbling. You want your hair to look pretty, don't you?" I nodded miserably.

"Tell me what you and Eira have been doing."

Eira was my best friend. She had dark, curly hair and this I envied.

"Eira is having a big, big doll's house for her birthday," I mumbled. This was an exaggeration.

"I wish I had a doll's house with a red roof and lace curtains on the windows," I sighed.

In silence Grandma finished her task and I turned to hug her and kiss her Goodnight. Cupping my face in her hands, she drew me so near that I could see the love in those brown eyes in the wrinkled face, as she said:

"Such a pale little face you've got, Hannah fach. Never you mind about Eira's doll's house. Wait until we get the Estate back in our family and you shall have the finest doll's house in the world."

I was to hear this many times. The Estate or "Y Stat" to me meant, 'When my ship comes in' and 'Chancery' was the wicked ogre who had stolen valuable property that belonged to Grandma's family by rights. They were convinced that Boverton Castle in the Vale of Glamorgan, with its vast estate, should have come to them, though the castle was a ruin long since and the estate in Chancery.

Patiently my father explained that the estate should go to 'male heirs for ever', and that Grandma and her brother were on the distaff side of the family, but she would not listen.

"My great, great, grandmother, Elizabeth Seys Pryce lived and died in Boverton Castle," she retorted, "but then, John Matthews, you are not one of the Pryces," and she flounced out of the kitchen at what, to her, was heresy.

I dreamed in a vague, romantic way about the estate and tried to imagine living in a castle, not in a small inn, and resented the way my father put a damper on Grandma's enthusiasm and my dreams.

Another parcel arrived, a big, bulky one from the Cash Hardware Shop.

"Quick, Dada, before Grandma sees it!" and like conspirators we carried the package into the parlour to unwrap. It contained two dozen rough linen glass-towels.

"Good girl," said my father, "just what I need. The beer comes tomorrow."

"What do you do with it Dada?" I asked.

"Bind the cask-stoppers, to strengthen them so that the beer won't leak. And it must be stiff or it's no good. See if your Grandma's about."

I darted into the passage. There was no sign of her. Luckily she was having a nap. Soon I heard my father hammering away and I knew he was in the cellar.

This was a dark, frightening place that smelled horribly of beer. Here I was able to peep, disgusted yet fascinated, when the beer-lorries stopped outside The Station Inn and the trap-door in the pavement was lifted up by the burly cask-handlers who looked like giants and reeked of beer, as did their soiled leather aprons. I felt one flap against my face as I stood on the pavement and peered into the depths of the cellar.

The men dropped two thick planks to lie, one end of each on the pavement, the other in the cellar and then the barrels were rolled down the planks and out of my sight.

Their work over, the men went into the bar for a free pint of beer. This room with its pungent smell of coke from the open stove in the middle, the sawdust scuffed about the floor from many feet and the smoky, beery atmosphere, held no charm for me. To get to our kitchen, there was no need to touch the 'business' part of the inn.

The front door opened on to a long, stone-flagged passage which ran straight through to the back door.

On the right of this passage were the bar, the snug for women customers and the large smoke-room. On the left of the passage lay the parlour which was private, and another small smoke-room. Few men used this room and here I was allowed to have my birthday parties.

We could walk through to the back door, across a small yard of paving-stones into the kitchen doors. So we had privacy.

It was only on Sundays that our front door was closed all day as The Station Inn was open from 6 a.m. until 11 p.m. on weekdays. I liked to sit on the doorstep and watch the trains rushing past, some slow trains, some fast expresses; all interesting.

There was more excitement for me one sunny day. Coming slowly up the road, but stopping to knock at every door, was a dark, sullen-faced woman. A basket hung on her arm and I knew she was a gipsy selling clothes-pegs; not the pale pointed ones bound with strips of tin, but the fawn-coloured ones that looked like little armless figures.

She pushed past me and went straight into the bar.

At that moment, a flurry of rustling black skirt that swept the floor, filled the width of the narrow passage as Grandma hurried towards me. The gipsy was coming out of the bar, so I flattened myself against the door as I knew what to expect from such a confrontation.

"And what do you want in the men's bar, I should like to know?" Grandma demanded.

The gipsy's earrings dangled as she nodded towards her basket.

"Not today, thank you" said Grandma firmly, "And I'd have you know women aren't allowed in the rooms where the men drink. Come, and I'll take you to the snug."

The woman shook her head.

"No, I don't want no drink. Buy some pegs, lady," she said ingratiatingly, "And your luck will be astounding," adding in a wheedling voice, "If you cross my palm with silver."

"Rubbish," said Grandma, but I was tugging at her full, black sleeve.

"Please, Grandma, buy some pegs," I pleaded.

"I don't need any. I've got plenty," said Grandma, brushing my hand from her sleeve.

"But not this sort. Look!" and I took a peg and held it up. "See, I can crayon the top for a face and put some ribbon or something for a dress, and it's a dolly."

"Oh, very well," and Grandma fetched some money from the pocket hidden in the deep folds of her skirt.

The woman counted the pennies, spat on them and put them in her drab little purse under the pegs. She patted me on the head with her dirt-ingrained hand, that smelled of paraffin, gave me a dazzle of white teeth, and I was dragged along to the kitchen by Grandma, as if she feared I might be snatched away to the gipsy tents for evermore.

****

It was before I was old enough to attend school that an earth tremor shook South Wales. I remember a jug falling off the dresser and would have been glad if the bottle of horrid medicine I had to take for anaemia had been smashed, but that stood on a low shelf and was unharmed.

The kitchen window looked on to the back gardens of houses down the street. It was always exciting to fetch the enamel rice-pudding dish with its scraps of bread and meat and to be lifted by Grandma through the window to take it to the chickens at the bottom of one of these gardens. I was usually rewarded with a sweet or an orange by the old grandmother of the house. One morning she asked me into the kitchen to wait while she washed the dish and persuaded me to sit at the table while she prepared some toast. I was fascinated to see her holding the long fork with a slice of thick bread on its prongs in front of the fire, her face a bright scarlet from the heat. She put the toast on the deal table, then, using the knife-handle, she carefully crushed the crust, so that it became soft enough for me to eat. Not a bit was wasted.

Seeing my interest, she gave me a piece, well-buttered, which I thought delicious and I decided to try this method at home.

"Look at the mess you are making, and whatever for?" Grandma asked, picking up the toast from the pile of crumbs, and she cut off the crust, but it didn't taste nearly as nice.

As The Station Inn was closed on Sundays it was given a thorough cleaning: scrubbing of flagged floors and polishing of furniture and brassware, which gleamed everywhere. My parents having gone to the evening service in the chapel, and my brother Dick put to bed, Grandma and I spent our quiet, happy evening hours together. The kitchen was my private little world, cut off from the public part of the house by a latched door which had a thick leather strap fixed low down so that we children could pull the door shut when we were too small to reach the latch.

The room was warm from cooking the dinner and the oven still hot.

"Go into the brew-house and find two nice, rosy apples, Hannah fach," Grandma said, and I knew there was a treat in store. Other children had a scullery where cooking and washing-up were done, but we had a brew-house: used long ago for brewing beer, I suppose. Filled with cored apples and lots of brown sugar, fine as sand, with a knob of butter on the top of each apple, the dish, with a drop of water to prevent burning, was put in the oven to bake very slowly. We chatted on the 'sciw' where, under the cushion, Grandma kept my hated curling-papers, and she would show me how to make spills out of narrow strips of newspaper. On Monday morning these were placed in empty tobacco tins in the smoke-rooms, where customers could light their pipes and cigarettes, and in the bar with its open coal-stove. The pipes which were sold in the bar were of white pipe-clay and there was always one each for Dick and me to make soap-bubbles. They cost, I think, a halfpenny each.

We always had Sunday dinner in the smoke-room adjoining the kitchen. This would be transformed into a cosy living-room for one day each week: the hearth's roaring fire, the gleaming brass fire-irons and a snowy table-cloth on the table that, the evening before, had borne dominoes, pints of beer and glasses of stout and spirits.

"This is the middle-kitchen, not a smoke-room," Grandma said as we ate. "Remember that."

After dinner, while Grandma and my mother went to bed for a rest, the cloth cleared away, my father's books and papers were spread before him and he started his writing. He was an insurance agent. If it was too wet for Sunday School, which was some distance away and needing a tram journey, time would drag. I used to worry my father for a penny, tugging at his coat until I heard his usual command:

"Close your eyes and see what God will give you."

Eagerly I obeyed, waiting to feel the penny being dropped into my hand and his fist closing my fingers over the coin. But it wasn't a penny at all; just a penny-shaped peppermint sweet, which made me mad as he knew very well I didn't like them. He played this trick on me time and again, but I was always caught by it.

On warm Sunday evenings my mother took Dick and me to chapel. There were always many mothers in the congregation, carrying quite small babies. There was no such thing as a baby sitter in those days and it wasn't considered unhygienic to take young children to church. There were always grandmothers happy to look after those left at home.

Grandma always gave us a halfpenny each to put in the collection plate. Dick soon grew sleepy in the warm atmosphere and climbed onto my mother's knee. Clutching his halfpenny in his fat little hand he was soon fast asleep, which gave me the chance I had been waiting for. I looked to see if mother was watching, but her eyes were intent on the preacher. Cunningly I eased Dick's halfpenny out of his sleep-slackened hand and when the deacon came round it was Dick's halfpenny that I put on the plate. I kept mine to spend on sweets on Monday. I did this many times before I was found out and made to feel a real criminal by Grandma.

Babies were held in their mothers' arms in the old Welsh fashion: a large shawl was placed over her shoulder, tucked round the baby held close to her breast, then the rest of the shawl brought tightly round the mother's back, under her other arm and across the front, the end fitting snugly under the bulge of the baby's body.

Fathers weren't ashamed to be seen carrying babies like this as they walked along the streets.

CHAPTER TWO

"There. Doesn't he look sweet?" and Grandma kissed and hugged my four-year old brother in the new suit my mother had made for him. "It's a pity Mama hasn't finished your new dress too; but never mind, Hannah fach, it will be ready by next Sunday."

Grandma's words had no effect on my disappointment at not having my new dress to wear. There Dick stood, being fussed over in the white blouse with huge navy-blue collar and tiny white trousers, ready to come with me to Sunday School. Hand in hand we walked along the road, quite a long walk; he, happy in his new suit and me - jealous because my dress was one I had worn several times before, although it was pretty.

It started to rain and before we reached the chapel there were puddles in the road. Suddenly I gave Dick a push and he fell sprawling in the mud, ruining his white suit. We walked dejectedly home.

As Grandma undressed him and washed his muddied face and hands she threw me a suspicious look when I explained "He fell in the mud," but in her wisdom she didn't utter a word of reproof. I expect she understood a child's temptation to do such a spiteful thing.

Soon my new dress was finished and we were taken to a photographer's, Dick in his suit, washed clean as new and me in the prettiest frock I had ever had. For some reason he was put to sit on a stuffed horse; a very unnatural horse it was too. With his mouth open, Dick looked terrified while I stood, my hand on the arm of a chair, looking very worried with my head to one side, a habit I have to this day.

There were never any dull moments for me at The Station Inn. I just had to run to the front door to watch the trains racing past on their way to London and their interested passengers who sometimes waved to the little girl outside the inn across the roadway. It was fun to wait for the train to appear, then run to the bottom of the road where Mrs. Bowen lived in the end house, in a futile attempt to race the galloping monster.

The day Grandma bought me a pair of red felt bedroom slippers was a happy one, and I wore them throughout the day. It was sheer bliss to tear along the pavement in those soft, kindly, foot-hugging slippers, keeping a wary eye on my competitor, the Fishguard-London express. Then I would stop at Mrs. Bowen's door to watch it disappear, its thundering noise lessening to a sigh, and it had gone; but never mind, there were plenty of trains running every day.

When Grandma's false teeth, which were so ghostly white they couldn't possibly be natural, gave her trouble, she would give up eating solid food and resort to 'Shenkin Esmwyth' which means 'Easy or smooth Jenkin'. This was bread and butter cut into small pieces, put into a bowl, sprinkled with brown sugar, then enough tea to cover, with milk added until it was a fawn colour. No one knew what Jenkin had to do with its name unless it was a man of that name who invented the dish when his mouth was sore.

We were thrilled when we heard that my father was going to take us to see the 'Pathricks', as it meant the excitement of watching a procession with a brass band. I didn't realise it was March 17, St. Patrick's Day, when all Swansea Irish marched down the High Street wearing their shamrocks, proudly showing our Welsh town who they were.

To be sure of getting into town, we took the train instead of the tram, which might be packed. Then we made our way to a good spot for seeing everything, where the window-sill of a public house in High Street seemed a splendid place. Seated here, our arms around my father's shoulders, we could see beautifully.

Just before the blaring music warned us of the approaching band, the very band in which a man known as "George Bach y Band" (Little George of the Band) who lived near The Station Inn would be playing his trumpet, a very tall man pushed his way through the crowd and stood right in front of us, utterly blocking the view. In temper, my little brother shot out his foot, kicking the man's bowler hat into the middle of the procession, to be probably kicked along like a football. The man went for my father and there was a fierce argument. I don't know whether or not my father offered to pay for the hat, as Dick started howling and we had to take him into a toyshop which had a huge rocking-horse in the window. It was terribly expensive and my father wasn't going to pay all that money for a toy for a naughty boy, and Dick had to be satisfied with a small wooden horse on wheels.

In spite of Grandma's warning that behind the kitchen door was not a good place for a stable, my brother insisted on carefully stabling his horse there before going to bed every night.

Before the week was out he disgraced himself again. One of the chapel deacons called to see Grandma who hadn't been well enough to attend chapel, and she suggested that he might like to see Dick's new horse. Eagerly the horse was produced but immediately we were all shocked as Dick flung the creature on the floor crying "It's no good. The damn thing's broke!"

That he should swear like that and in front of Mr. John too! Where had he learnt such language? Where indeed, when we lived in a public house, and how many bad words had come to our innocent young ears from the "Business?"

I was about seven years of age when Grandma took me to

Kingsbridge, a few miles out of Swansea. She said to my mother, "Cassie, it's time I went to see how things are in the old home, and I'll take Hannah fach with me."

So off we set, first by train, then by trap, to the inn where my mother had spent her childhood with Grandma, Grandpa and mother's only sister, Auntie Sally.

The train journey was exciting. A woman in our compartment had a small boy with her, warmly wrapped up, and she insisted on having the window open while the train went through a tunnel, holding him near the window so that he could inhale the horrid fumes. She said this was good for his whooping-cough, but it was very unpleasant for us and the others in the compartment. It was a relief when the train journey was over.

Sitting later in a pony-trap I clutched at Grandma wildly, expecting to be flung out onto the road any minute. The trap jolted along for a mile or so and we arrived at The Kingsbridge Inn.

The inn had been leased to a family who were supposed to keep everything in good condition. We didn't receive much of a welcome from the landlady as we walked through the rooms, where Grandma cast a suspicious eye everywhere. Then we went into the garden. Here, Grandpa had grown his beloved flowers. To Grandma's dismay there was no flower garden to be seen; all had been given over to vegetables. She looked about her sadly.

"It's a good thing your grandfather didn't live to see this day" she said, and this remark told me a little about him. He had died before I was born and Grandma's words set me wondering about my mother's childhood in this village inn, and I could hardly wait to ask her all about it.

It was a free house, which meant that beer and spirits could be bought at any brewery. Consequently Grandma and Grandpa were treated with great respect by the brewers who wished to keep their custom. Every Christmas they were given presents; a huge turkey and goose, a pair of fine kid gloves for Grandma and a bottle of port for Grandpa. When the representative called for the money he would spend a long time chatting with Grandma, who was obviously the 'boss'. Their servant, Mary Ann brought in a drink for him but nothing for Grandma, who disapproved of women drinking but she always allowed him to offer Mary Ann one.

"She will have a glass of rum," she would say without consulting Mary Ann and in a few minutes the smiling servant reappeared with a large glass of rum.

"Your respects, sir, and thank you. I'll drink it later." Smiles all round as she bore off the rum and the sixpence to the kitchen where she pocketed the coin and poured the drink down the sink. It was, of course, not rum but cold tea. Grandma didn't allow her to take strong drink and the money came in useful towards

Mary Ann's bottom drawer.

My grandparents were faithful members of the local Baptist chapel and, when ministers were engaged to preach at the Anniversary Meetings it was at The Kingsbridge Inn that they stayed. It was one of these men, famous in the Baptist denomination who said, out of his deep regard for Grandma's character:

"SHE OUGHT TO BE IN THE PULPIT, NOT THE PUB!"

A river ran at the bottom of the garden of The Kingsbridge Inn, and when my mother was baptised at the age of twelve it was in this very river that the ceremony took place.

Later, sitting in the trap with Grandma on our way to the station for our homeward journey, she said, her eyes filled with sad memory:

"Your grandfather was too ill to go to the riverside for the service so he sat in his bedroom with the window open so that he could hear the hymn-singing which was carried up the river on the breeze."

I thought that a lovely idea, but was sure I'd have been terrified of being immersed in cold water, especially in a pebbly river. Pointing to the right, Grandma continued "Look. Over there, you can just see the river and the back of The Kingsbridge Inn," pointing in the direction of the inn now fast receding into a toy house in the distance.

"That's the window where my husband, your grandfather, John Daniel, sat listening."

We were almost at the station when she added wistfully, "Sometimes they had to break the ice on the river for a baptism in winter," which sounded more terrifying still.

We had the window closed all the way back, but we could still smell the heavy smoke as the train raced through the tunnel. The woman and her little boy were not on the train, which was, so Grandma said, a good thing.

All I learned of my grandfather came from my mother, who told me he wasn't a godly man on the face of it; that is, he had to be coaxed by Grandma into attending the chapel services. He spent many hours in the large garden in his oldest clothes and here he was utterly happy.

"One day," said my mother, "he was missing for hours and when asked where he had been he replied:

"Only to Swansea to buy a new rake for the garden."

"What. Like that?" cried Grandma crossly. "You look like a tramp."

"Never mind. No one knows me in Swansea so what does it matter?"

Another day he got away with a crafty excuse after disappearing for a long time. Still wearing his gardening clothes he walked into the inn and said he'd been to the village.

Grandma was furious.

"John Daniel, you've disgraced me. In our own village, too! Who saw you?"

"Everybody I expect," he replied coolly. "Anyway, they all know me there so what's all the fuss about? They know I've got better, as I wear a tidy suit to go to chapel, don't I?"

Grandma was defeated again by this piece of logic.

Grandpa's love of flowers was such that he hated to see people wearing them. He maintained that human beings weren't worthy of wearing such God-given things of beauty.

In Swansea market bunches of vegetables were bought for making broth; they were tied together by their stems with string and, shining out among the brown of swede and onion, the white of turnip and dull red of carrot, a bright orange sprig of marigold. This was added to the broth for extra flavour.

Grandpa didn't enjoy his broth when he saw these petals floating on top, and once when he caught a servant throwing some dead flowers on the kitchen fire he was very angry. Almost burning his hands as he picked them from the blaze, he said, "Flowers are beautiful things that have lived. They have a kind of soul and mustn't be treated as rubbish."

I decided I liked my dead grandfather who thought so kindly about flowers. Some years later, I found among the pages of Grandma's big, black Bible, a poem he had written in Welsh under a pen-name 'Ap Mawrth' (Son of March). I concluded rightly that he was born in March.

"What did he think of the chances the Pryce family had of regaining the estate?" I asked.

"Well," said my mother, "although it wasn't his own family, he knew all about it from Grandma. In fact, one day he went on impulse up to the large mansion which, so she claimed, should have come to her family. The present owner had no right to be living there. Your grandfather marched up that long drive to the house" my mother said dramatically, "and when the butler answered his loud knocking, he blurted out, 'This house by rights should belong to my wife's family, the Pryces. The present owner has no title deeds and I demand to see what documents he has in his strong room concerning his claim'."

Although I admired my grandfather's courage, I wasn't surprised when mother concluded, "He was told to clear off and the door was slammed in his face."

MY GRANDFATHER.

He died
long before I was born, yet I knew
his gentle spirit: felt, still feel
his presence close beside
me. Interested
when my poised uncertain pen,
seeking a truly bardic phrase, hesitated.
In eagerness to help, his thoughts flew
into mine. They said he signed
"Ap Mawrth" beneath his simple verse.
June-soft they were, like flower-
petals, unlike his gusty birthmonth wind.
Tending his garden satisfied his every leisure hour.
On seeing faded dahlias roughly thrown
upon the kitchen fire, sad-eyed
he'd grasped them: finger-singed, laid them down
on the cool stone floor, gently like a nurse.
"They too have souls of a kind,"
he had explained to her who sinned.
His faith in this was real.
From Mother's gown
he had unpinned
the morning freshly-picked pink rosebud spray.
"We humans are unworthy of their wearing,"
had been his mild rebuke. "You
should have left it where it grew,"
In silent protest he would shun
The bowl of broth where marigold petals, floating
lay,
added for flavour by some uncaring
one. This was my grandfather's kindly way.

H. Doris Williams, Swansea.

Ap Mawrth. (Son of March)

CHAPTER THREE

I have mentioned my cousins who lived with us at The Station Inn, so I must introduce the others and explain why we were all living there together, 'Like Brown's Cows', as Grandma might say.

My Auntie Sally, short for Sarah, was married when a young girl of seventeen, 'with her hair hanging down her back', when they were living at The Kingsbridge Inn. Auntie Sally was eleven years older than my mother. The son of a local rector fell in love with my aunt, and no wonder, as she was so pretty.

Glyn, the young man, was still at public school, and the rector didn't at all approve of his son marrying so young and to the daughter of a publican at that; but in the end he saw the couple were very much in love and agreed to the marriage.

Uncle Glyn had as yet no profession, and any plans of a career for him were out of the question as he was now a married man with responsibilities to shoulder. He must have had a very fine character and I was very moved when Grandma told me that he had been known to give his coat, or rather 'the coat off his back' to a beggar. But what drew my admiration was an account of his swimming across a river and being able to shoot in the air at the same time. I couldn't imagine such dexterity but it sounded very clever and I wanted to believe every word of it.

When Grandma, Grandpa and my mother moved to The Station Inn, Landore, where I was born, the young couple took over The Kingsbridge Inn which, I suspect, my uncle was quite unsuited to run. Here their three children, Claudia, Ethel and Trevor were born. Uncle Glyn died soon after Ethel was born and Auntie Sally and the girls came to live at The Station Inn with Grandma, while the rector, as might be expected, took the boy Trevor to live at the rectory, where he was brought up like a 'proper gentleman'. There he had a nanny, a governess, went to public school and 'did a trip round the world before he was twenty', Grandma would say with pride. That he was called 'Boysie' at the rectory displeased Grandma, who always called him 'Trevor' on his visits.

When I was told of his escapade on his last day at public school I thought him quite a hero, though Grandma said he was just a naughty boy, "Carving his name on the lid of his desk and a full-rigged sailing ship if you please."

"Was he punished?" I asked her, "Or didn't they find out?" She couldn't tell me, but I hoped they didn't, or if they had, that it wasn't a very severe caning or whatever headmasters did for that crime.

My mother said they never knew when to expect Trevor, even from as far away as Africa or Australia. One day when she was busy she felt a strong pair of arms round her waist and she was being swung round, to face Trevor, home from Africa where he had been wild-game hunting. I longed to meet this intrepid hunter who surely would have wonderful stories to tell, but that wasn't to be for several years.

It was inevitable that Auntie Sally would marry again, this time to a Scotsman by whom she had several children. They went away to keep an inn somewhere in Wales. I never knew where, and when Auntie Sally died, two of her daughters by this marriage came to live with us. So there we were: my parents, Evelyn, Dick and myself, Claudia and Ethel of Auntie's first marriage and Ray and Gwen of her second; all of us under Grandma's roof and loving care.

The half-sisters weren't alike. Claudia and Ethel were fair-skinned with auburn hair, while Ray and Gwen were dark with brown hair and eyes. Ray had a Roman nose which was considered to be aristocratic. Gwen's eyes were very striking, like pools of black liquid. There was a younger daughter, Olive, who when her mother died went to live with her father.

Claudia went to London as a nurse at Great Ormond Street Hospital, so it was only after her return to Landore and subsequent marriage that I saw much of her, as she lived a walkable distance away. But Ethel was more like a sister to me. She was really beautiful with unusual colouring, her eyes being brown, her cheeks pink and white and her hair a rich auburn.

Ethel went to a private school where she contracted a germ which took away all her hair. This was very embarrassing for her as all young girls wore their hair long, so Grandma bought her a wig. Fortunately her hair soon grew again into a crown of curls.

When she was old enough she served in the bar and was so modest that when customers stared at her, struck by her rare beauty, she blushed, thinking she looked untidy. On Monday mornings, when she helped the woman who came to do the washing, Ethel was a picture. Her hair was like a halo of flat little rings along her forehead from the steam from the boiler in the brewhouse. She was a sunny soul and would whistle as she pegged the clothes on the line, just like Ronnie Ronalde on the radio.

Ethel rather bossed us, as she was very house-proud, and I confess to being cheeky to her when I was told off for walking into the clean kitchen in my muddy feet. "My feet are clean; it's my shoes that are dirty," I retorted.

Ethel had a friend, a colliery manager of whom Grandma approved as he was a member of our chapel. It was exciting the day he took her down into his colliery, all those hundreds of feet underground, an experience I would love to have shared, but I suppose I was too young and would have been 'de trop' anyway.

This colliery was unique in that the miners had requested that a chapel be made, over seven hundred feet below ground, so that they could hold a prayer-meeting at the commencement of each week. A rustic pulpit was built between the timber posts near the pit shaft. These posts were white lime-washed to give an appearance of spaciousness in the cramped, primitive setting.

Candles each side of the pulpit formed the only lighting, as the colliers on entering put out their lamps which they hung on the roughly-made benches. Some hung their lamps on their 'Yorks', the name given to the leather trouser strap fastened below the knee, a kind of garter. The service began with a hymn, followed by a bible reading and a prayer, then a closing hymn. The overflow meeting joined lustily in the singing. The pit horses weren't allowed to be harnessed until after the service had ended and the bible put away for safety until the following Monday morning at seven o'clock.

Several years after this event I heard a B.B.C. recording of one of these services and could well imagine the scene.

Grandma wasn't to have her own matchmaking way over Ethel's friendship with the colliery manager, and Ethel married another young man whom we all liked. I noticed, young as I was, that she used to twitch her hands, especially if you looked straight at her for a few moments. Grandma explained it was St. Vitus Dance and that I mustn't remark on it in Ethel's hearing.

She was married very quietly owing to this nervous habit and lived with us until her sudden illness, when she was rushed to hospital. Having overheard my parents' hushed conversations I concluded that Ethel was pregnant and tried to connect it all with St. Vitus Dance. The following days were agony for me as I recalled over and over again all I had done to displease her. The kitchen accused me. How often had Ethel to tell me off for walking on the freshly-scrubbed flagstones without wiping my feet!

"Put your goloshes in the brewhouse and hang up your coat!" And I had ignored her commands. Frantically I prayed "Please, God, don't let Ethel die! Make her better and I promise I'll never be cheeky to her again." I sat, limply, on the chair by the kitchen door, my cheek damply against the mahogany bookcase.

During that ghastly week, the very air seemed to move on tiptoe through the house. At the end of the week Ethel died. It had seemed more like a month and we wished longingly that we lived in a proper private house where every room could share, as it were, our sorrow. But we lived in an inn and the 'business' must be re-opened after a couple of days according to the licensing laws, and life must go on. The noises of the public part of the inn was a cruel affront to our feeling of great loss and deep sadness.

A cable was sent to Trevor in Africa but it was impossible for him to come home in time for the funeral.

****

Friday was 'bread-day' at home. In the morning, Lizzie our servant always made bread in the huge round earthenware pan. This tapered to the bottom and was glazed on the inside and dull on the outside. There would be a roaring fire in the kitchen and the pan would be placed in front of it, covered with a linen cloth so that the dough could rise. As we came down the ramp from the inn-yard, through the kitchen door we could smell the delicious baking-smell. Magically it seemed the dough had risen while we were in school and it had been kneaded and placed in tins. Sometimes we saw Lizzie's strong, red hands punching the dough and shaping it into oblongs to put in the tins. When I pointed out that the tins weren't full enough, Grandma explained that the dough would rise more again when being baked.

"Now, Hannah fach, here's the knife. Cut a nice big 'D' for Daniel in the middle." This I could do by myself as I was seven years old.

"Come on, Dick bach. It's your turn next,"and, with her hand guiding his fat little one, another 'D' was cut.

"D' for Dick," she said smiling, and this he really believed.

On our way to school we had to carry the bread to the baker's for baking. I carried one tin of dough under each arm, Dick carried one and Lizzie the remaining tins in a big basket. My sister Evelyn attended a private school in Swansea, so she got out of this job. On our way home from school we picked up three loaves and we couldn't resist picking the little bits of crust off the top to eat.

****

My beloved Miss Padden, my teacher, was a psychologist if ever there was one. She knew how painfully shy I was. When told to stand up in class to respond to a question I let her think I didn't know the answer rather than speak in that husky little voice I had; but if she persisted "Do you know the answer?" I would nod my head eagerly.

"Then come out to my desk and whisper it in my ear."

On Friday afternoons, after playtime, we had 'Silent Reading' and Miss Padden would take from her desk a big bag of boiled sweets. Forty pairs of greedy eyes peeped over books as she tore a large sheet of tissue paper into little pieces, large enough to wrap round a sweet. Eventually an exciting-looking pile lay on her desk and we were called out, one by one, to stand along the glass partition separating our classroom from the next one. With hands behind our backs we tried hard to look good, each hoping to be the first to be given a sweet. When all were in line we sang 'Now the day is over' and Miss Padden called us up to her desk for a sweet. Every child had one, every Friday, but it was a special thrill to be the first one chosen. I made a point of offering my sweet to Grandma, which wasn't so unselfish as it sounds, as I knew perfectly well that she didn't like sweets.

It was heartbreaking when I was put up a class because I was eight years old and had to leave Miss Padden. I was prepared to hate my new teacher who couldn't possibly be as kind as Miss Padden. There was little comfort in realising that she was there behind the glass partition, and when standing on tip-toe I could just see her grey hair as she wrote on the blackboard. It was unfortunate that shortly after entering my new class I was away from school for three weeks with a badly-burned leg. When reaching for the teapot on the hob of the kitchen fireplace I tipped it and the scalding tea ran all over my leg. Lizzie was sent to the butcher's for some white stringy fat which Grandma called 'pig's fleek, good for burns' and this she bandaged round my leg. I rather enjoyed being fussed over by Grandma, who got my father to cut a walking stick for me to use. But when I was well enough to return to school it was to face this new teacher. What about all the lessons I had missed? Recitation time came and we had to stand up in turn. When my time came I couldn't say a word!

"Go on, child, recite 'Florence Nightingale'," the teacher said. I was mute, as I hadn't been in school when they had learned the poem.

"A lady with a lamp I see,"she prompted sharply and waited.

"Now go on." Miserably I explained.

"Well, see that you learn it by next week," her cold voice commanded and then and there I determined that when I grew up I would marry and bring my husband to the school to give her a good hiding. It didn't occur to me then that she might be retired and married with children of her own.

A weakling, I found myself missing a good deal by being at home ill and at the age of nine spent many months away from school, feeling languid and pitifully pale and thin. My hair was uninterestingly fair beside my washed-out blue eyes.

I spent much of the time with my friend Eira who was very delicate and we used to lie in her garden for hours in the sun. Here we decided to plant a flower-patch in the shape of a heart, having bought a packet of seeds which we sprinkled to form, we hoped, our initials, expecting blooms like those on the packet, but all that came up were weeds.

On wet days we sat in Eira's kitchen with its Welsh dresser that had no back to it, which meant it was a genuine antique. Between the shelves that held lustre jugs you could see the wallpaper. But what charmed me most were the two small cupboards, one on top of the other, beside the fireplace. The bottom one had an oak door but the top had a glass door with a white muslin curtain across it. I wondered what there might be behind that curtain. It could be a lovely room in a fairy palace or a doll's house, though Eira never said anything about it. My imagination was keyed up about that cupboard until the day her mother opened it while laying the tea. I was bursting with excitement. All was revealed; it was just a cupboard with cups and saucers of white china with tiny blue flowers. The dainty cups hung from hooks on the shelves. My dream was shattered.

CHAPTER FOUR

Not far away from The Station Inn there was a chapel which Grandma called 'Capel y Gwlaw' (the rain chapel), as when it was too wet for people to get to their own chapels, they went there. Here, once a week a children's concert was held, which we wouldn't miss. It was a simple affair; children of the Sunday School recited poems, which were invariably sad and made me cry, or sang sacred songs, and teachers told us interesting stories.

Grandma willingly gave me the penny for the concert as it was in a chapel, and Eira's mother gave her one; but we had a problem here as we had a friend whom I shall call Shirley who never had a penny, so we paid for her. It was definitely a loan which Shirley promised to repay. Getting the extra halfpenny was difficult as Grandma would offer me sweets from her supply, but she gave in in the end. As Eira's mother kept a grocer's shop where they sold sweets, the offer of a bar of 'Five Boys' chocolate was hard to refuse. She demanded:

"What do you want another halfpenny for, when we have plenty of sweets in the shop? Spending my money in another shop indeed!" Though grudgingly, the money was given at last and we three set off. It was when the debt had reached threepence owed to Eira and threepence owed to me that we rebelled. You could buy heaps of sweets for threepence and we had paid for six concerts for Shirley. So on the Friday evening, when we knew her father had his wages at the docks where he worked, we timidly approached Shirley's house.

"Please will you pay us the money you owe us?" was the speech we rehearsed as we climbed up the steps to the front door. We hoped Shirley's mother, a forbidding-looking woman, wouldn't open it and to our relief it was Shirley herself, who said her father wasn't home yet and suggested that we went to meet him. Determined to get the money we walked half way to Swansea it seemed, but didn't meet him. He had gone home another way and we felt sure we had been tricked and that Shirley knew all along.

One of our teachers left school to get married, and Eira and I weren't content with contributing towards a present from the children: we insisted on our parents buying a personal gift, not anything expensive, but it gave us great pleasure to do so. Shirley heard of this and wanted to do the same but, knowing her mother would never spend money on such a thing, took an ornament from the top of the chest of drawers in their parlour. Happily we three went to school the next morning with our wedding gifts, but Shirley's pleasure was short-lived as her mother had discovered the theft and marched up to school to confront the poor teacher, demanding the ornament back. It was lying on the teacher's desk with all the other little individual gifts. Suddenly the door burst open and in marched Shirley's mother. Without a word to the teacher she grabbed the little 'coat of arms of Swansea' ornament and, snorting, took it away. All eyes were fixed on the accusing gap among the gifts.

Although Shirley had little pocket-money, her parents were known to be rich; in fact they had 'rows of houses in the bank'. One morning in the holidays she asked Eira and me to help collect rents for her mother. We went along, little knowing the reception we were to have. The houses were part of a row of very small, shabby houses where the women stood outside gossiping. Eira and I were taken aback as we walked up to the first house for the rent as the woman glared at Shirley and shouted,

"Don't come here asking for rent. Tell your mother to mend this roof!" Eira and I shrank back, but Shirley wasn't so sensitive and stood her ground until the woman went indoors, slamming it fiercely behind her. Within minutes, all the other tenants had disappeared too. As we walked home, Eira and I told Shirley never to ask US to go collecting rents with her again.

But one of the tenants had a part-time job at a cinema which was quite a long, hilly walk from Landore, and apart from doing some repairs to his own house he offered also to allow Shirley and her friends free admission to the cinema on Saturday afternoons in lieu of rent arrears. We jumped at this chance and, as he let us in at the entrance, wearing a commissionaire's uniform, he gave us bars of chocolate to eat inside and led us to good seats. During one sad film in which a little orphan boy lay huddled at the road side, the silence, disturbed only by the sniffles of the sympathetic young audience, was shattered by an old man crying out loudly,

"Poor little bugger!"

This relieved the situation as people began to laugh and the ache in my throat from trying to choke back my tears was giving me a headache.

These jaunts ended when the commissionaire was dismissed for letting friends in free and stealing chocolate.

When Grandma found out where we'd been on Saturday afternoons, making me so tired at tea-time, she was disgusted.

"Serves you right!" she said. "Walking all that way for something for nothing. Dishonest, that's what it is.

****

My father suffered severely from asthma, so he spent much of his time sitting down and looking after things generally and he became very stout. On Dick's first day at school we were playing in the schoolyard when we saw my father outside the railings and ran to talk to him. He had come to see how Dick was facing up to his new life and relieved that I was taking care of him. I was only seven, but remember thinking "Why is Dada so fat?" My mother was always too busy to put on weight and I was aware of a feeling of unfairness in this order of things, especially when I had a chest cold. It was always my father who rubbed the camphorated oil on my chest, the palms of my hands and the soles of my feet; never my mother. Her hands were too rough from handling beer. She would pamper my father, always explaining how he suffered from asthma. I can see her now, holding her hand on her breast,

"Jack's chest is so tight," and when asked how she was herself, laughingly replied "I haven't time to be ill. There's so much to do." That was why, I suppose, Grandma took over the mothering of me in many ways.

Sometimes when Eira and I were playing in the park she would suddenly stop and say, for no obvious reason except perhaps that the sky threatened a storm: "I hope my mother is all right. Come on, let's go home." But when we reached her house her mother and aunt were perfectly well and I felt "I must be a nasty girl: I never worry if Mama's all right." On one occasion I too, following Eira's example, ran home, only to find my mother up to her eyes in work at the bar, impatient at seeing me hovering around her anxiously and wondering why on earth I had come home instead of playing out of doors until the last minute, as I usually did.

I came home from school one dinner-time and saw our odd-job man Billy having dinner in the kitchen. He was a very popular old man who invariably spoke in Welsh, but this day I heard him say three words in English. The incident impressed me so deeply that I have never forgotten it and it is described in the following poem, published some time ago:-

"OLD BILLY - A CHARACTER"

I, a child came home from school at
dinner-time: paused at the kitchen-door,
watched our odd-job man Billy who sat
hunched at the table, finishing the dinner
given him for shifting a stack of coal.
His vacant face intent, he scraped the plate
with bread, held in dirt-ingrained fingers
for the last trace of gravy.
Unaware of me, his eyes rolled briefly upwards
as he muttered, "THANK YOU, GOD,"
wiped a forgiven hand across his slack mouth,
grabbed from the floor his dirty cap,
slapped it on his bald head and slouched past me
into the sunshine, and his next job.

One morning I noticed that the girl sitting behind me in class was wearing the prettiest brooch I had ever seen. There were two dancing figures in brightly-coloured enamel, a boy and a girl in gipsy costume, holding hands. I longed to have one like it but Grandma didn't encourage us to wear jewellery. "Balchder" (pride or vanity) was a sin.

When the bell was rung at the end of playtime and we were running to our lines, I saw the brooch on the ground. I picked it up, put it in my handkerchief and held it tightly in my hand. For the remainder of that morning I sat in my desk clutching the brooch with a desire to possess I have never known since. And all the time I could almost feel a pair of accusing eyes boring into my guilty back; perhaps tearful eyes at having lost the precious thing. But I couldn't keep it up. Just before hometime I slipped out and gave the brooch to Miss Padden, who held it up asking if anyone in our class had lost it. When I saw Millie put her hand up to her collar, I realised she hadn't missed it. She took it gratefully from Miss Padden and threw me a 'thank you' smile. My sense of relief from the burden of guilt was immense but the affair wasn't allowed to rest. What an honest little girl I was! Some children might have been tempted to keep the brooch, said Miss Padden. My cheeks burned and as I walked home from school at dinnertime I felt I'd been a thief in my heart at least. I didn't mention it to Grandma. She would have asked me why I didn't take it at once to its owner. I made up my mind to save up and buy a brooch exactly the same as the one I had nursed for a happy little while.

Except for Miss Padden, teachers were not friendly people in our eyes. They were stern, black-gowned women, their black sateen aprons spattered with chalk dust. They took all the heat from the coal fire by standing in front of it.

I was never warm enough in school and found that by sitting on my hands I could warm them. This was quickly noticed by my teacher.

"Stop screwing your face up like that, and stop wriggling!"

It was a relief when playtime came and I could run round the yard. I dreaded wet days as my curls drooped and my hair became quite straight, which brought a question from one of my class-mates which resulted in humiliation for me.

"Who curls your hair for you, Doris?"

"My grandma," I answered.

"Will she curl mine?" came a chorus from others who had gathered round.

"Of course," I said, feeling proud and quite sure she would.

When I opened the kitchen door after school that day, five

little girls stood right behind me, waiting to be invited in.

"What's this?" Grandma demanded.

"I've brought my friends for you to curl their hair like mine," I explained, motioning them to follow me.

"Certainly not," Grandma stormed, rolling her 'R' threateningly as she held them back. "Go home and get your own mothers to curl your hair," she said. And they ran off. I drew away from her loving kiss. I almost hated her then; I felt so ashamed.

****

Being put up a class meant having a new teacher, an ordeal I dreaded. One very worrying day the new teacher said,

"Sit up everybody and answer my questions. Hands behind." and we obediently did so.

"Where does your father work, Maggie?"

"In the tin-works, Miss Jones."

"Muriel?"

"In the steelworks."

"Mary?"

"In the colliery."

"Which one?"

"The Mynyddbach colliery." (The little mountain pit)

"Annie?"

"In the copperworks."

"Bessie?"

"In the spelter works."

"Nellie?"

"In the Mynydd Newydd Colliery." (The new mountain pit)

"Beatrice?"

"There was no reply from Beatrice.

"Didn't you hear me? Where does your father work?"

"In the steel works."

"Pay attention all of you and sit up straight. Hands on heads." This was a relief from 'Hands behind' anyway.

"Sarah?"

"In the oil works."

"What are you and Beatrice giggling about?" There was no reply but a silence full of threat filled the room.

"Stand up both of you. Now tell me what was so amusing." Haltingly Sarah said,

"I said, Miss, what if you said 'Hands on your behinds' instead of 'Hands on your heads."

No one dared even smile, though our thoughts flew to the ridiculous picture that would have made.

"Now. Where was I? Oh yes, Millie?"

"In the Mannesmann."

"I suppose you mean the Mannesmann Tube Works?" Millie nodded. Now it was my turn and I was very nervous.

"Doris?"

"I don't know."

"You don't know where your father works?" Miserably I shook my head.

"Come here, child." I went up to her desk, conscious of forty pairs of eyes on me. How I longed to be able to answer pat 'In the tin works' or, better still, 'In the Mannesmann Tube Works' which sounded so grand, but it wasn't true.

"Well, what does your father do?" Miss Jones asked sharply.

"He's in the bar, but on Sundays he has a lot of papers in the middle kitchen and he writes in a book."

"I see. You live in an inn and your father works in the bar?" I nodded.

"Then he's a licensed victualler." I noted she pronounced it 'vittler'. Grandma always pronounced it as it is spelt.

At that time my father was an insurance agent, but I was too young and nervous to attempt to explain this to my new teacher.

When I told Grandma she should say 'vittler' not 'victualler' she snorted,

"What was all that about?" and I had to tell her.

"Why didn't you say he is an insurance agent?"

"I was frightened. I didn't remember the word, but I did say he had a lot of papers and he wrote in a book on Sundays and that he worked in the bar and everything. Nearly all the other girls said their fathers worked in the works," I added moodily.

"It's a good thing your father doesn't work in the works with his bad chest, Hannah fach." She put down her darning.

"Do you know that every metal, even gold, is worked in Swansea?" This I found difficult to believe. Pointing to the gleaming model of a horse on the mantelpiece, she said

"It was your father's friend who works in the tinworks who made that for him."

The beautiful model shone in the firelight like silver, which I had thought it was until Grandma said it was 'block tin'.

"How could any working man afford a real silver horse even for a wedding present for his best friend?" she laughed and went on "But silver was worked in Swansea you know. Oh yes. And do you know, merch i (my girl) what the owners of the silver works found out?"

I couldn't imagine.

"Well," Grandma said with relish, "they noticed that silver was disappearing from the works, so they made a surprise visit to the homes of their workmen, and, if you please, what did they see on the mantelpieces?"

"Silver things, I suppose," I guessed.

"Yes, little silver horses they'd made from silver taken from the works. Not all the men were dishonest, but those that did steal the silver had to give every piece back to be melted down."

"Did they lose their jobs?"

"No. They were good workers and you can be sure they didn't try it on again."

I took our tin horse down. It was a dainty model of a trotting horse, ten inches long and seven high. With one foot raised it gave the impression of passing by. The hairs on the tail and mane were almost separate. Held in my hands it seemed very thin, though heavy, and I realised it was only a one-sided model of a horse.

It stood on the mantelpiece alongside the china cat which had been all white until the day Grandma caught me beginning to paint it black, 'for a change'. The paint box was at hand and I had just managed to paint the paws when I was stopped. Grandma said

"I don't want a black cat. It will remind me of poor old Major." He was the very old cat who had died at a great age and whom I never saw moving from the rug on the hearth.

The paint washed off easily.

"Lucky for you it isn't real paint,"grumbled Grandma. I didn't explain that water colours are real paint. It was best to escape.

I was glad we didn't have a dog as I was afraid of them, a fear inherited perhaps from my father who had had a nasty experience with a dog when courting mother. He had gone to see her father when the old man was laid up with illness. When he approached the bed, grandfather's dog Asca sprang at him, thinking no doubt that father was about to attack his master. My father was badly injured.

CHAPTER FIVE

My other grandmother was such a terrible tease she even made me cry. One day she saw me coming down the hill from school and a boy in my class happened to be walking alongside me. That was enough to set her off teasing me about him. She told everyone he was my sweetheart and the poor little boy was hardly aware of my existence I'm sure, but that teasing made me hate the sight of him ever after.

When we went to bed, we said our prayers aloud, starting with

"Please God, bless Mama and Dada, Grandma Daniel, Evelyn, Dick, Claudia, Ethel, Ray and Gwen." I paused. Grandma was as usual listening. Then I whispered,

"But not Grandma Matthews because she teases me."

Grandma told my mother, who told my father, who told his mother to whom it was hilariously funny and I was teased more than ever about the boy and especially about my prayer. I couldn't forgive Grandma for letting them all know. I didn't think you could say your prayers silently.

My two grandmothers were good friends and I remember one holiday they spent together. They were totally different in some ways. Grandma Daniel was stern and deeply religious, though with a keen sense of humour and a deep conviction that the estate would return to her family. Grandma Matthews was gentle and loving. She adored us children. Every morning as we set off for school she would stand on the doorstep of her house. The moment we drew near she would call out in happiness, her arms outreaching "Merch anwyl i, machgen anwyl i." (My darling girl, my darling boy), smothering us in kisses as if she hadn't seen us for a long time.

My father's youngest sister heard all this and came to the door.

"Hush! Mother, for goodness' sake, what will the neighbours think?"

It didn't matter what anyone thought and, even if it meant being late for school, Dick and I wouldn't dream of missing our morning greeting at Grandma Matthews's doorstep.

Sometimes I had to take a message to her from my father. Eira always came along too, and we both thought Grandma Matthews was terribly brave. We were sitting in her kitchen one cold evening before a roaring red fire when suddenly a large lump of red hot coal fell out on the hearth. Without pausing Grandma Matthews picked it up in her bare hands and threw it on top of the fire. We looked on in amazement and awe, thinking she had some wonderful gift to be able to do such a thing without burning herself.

Occasionally I was asked to sleep with her when her two

daughters were away on holiday. She would 'cwtch' (cuddle) me and be sweet to me in every way, knowing I would be missing my own bed. I lay awake early in the morning having been awakened by the heavy boots of men going to work and missing, too, the bustle of The Station Inn and all its occupants, especially Grandma Daniel. When I suffered from earache it was from Grandma Matthews's garden that we had the house-leek to cure it. My mother had to squeeze the juice from the fleshy leaves into my ear to ease the pain.

When Grandma Matthews came to The Station Inn, it was to tea. I never saw her or Grandma Daniel or my mother take a drop of intoxicating drink, even for illness.

"Strong drink is raging, wine is a mockers." often heard stated in the kitchen but it didn't strike me as hypocritical that we were being kept by the sale of strong drink. I thought the red wine in the bottles in the bar was brandy. I was surprised when told years later that it was port. Somehow brandy had a red sound.

Grandma Matthews wore her cap and bonnet to visit us and I don't think she wore a lace cap at home. Her grey hair was straight and drawn back into a bun just like Grandma Daniel and all other grandmothers I knew. She wore spectacles which she always seemed to be losing until she would find, on looking in the mirror, that she had pushed them up on to her hair out of the way when doing a job.

****

With the passing of years my father grew stouter and when I was much older and went to college in London, I noticed that other students' fathers who visited them were all tall, slim, and many in smart uniforms showing high rank.

It was too long a journey from Swansea to London for my father to visit me. I was secretly glad. Had my father strolled up that stately college drive I knew I would feel ashamed. Hadn't a visiting lecturer said that the Greeks demanded physical as well as mental fitness before a man could be considered cultured or educated? One of our lady lecturers was very plump and I noticed how she blushed as he added, "If a fat man walked down the street, people might remark, 'What an uneducated man!", not 'What a stout man!'

But all this was in the future. In the meantime, my father, blue-eyed with a heavy brown moustache that hid a well-shaped mouth, was always ready to be run to in time of trouble. There was comfort in resting my head against his paunchy stomach even though I could feel the gold chain and 'Albert' (gold pendant) that dangled, pressing uncomfortably on my cheek. Eira loved my father too, her father having died when she was little more than a baby and my father was always ready to listen to our childish woes and to make us laugh.

He taught me how to read music from tonic solfa, which my mother never understood: and how to do the 'hand-signs' for the scale, which I can only describe as closing the fist for one note, pointing a finger upwards for another, downwards for another and holding the open hand up, down or sideways for yet other notes. All these he showed me, singing the scale as he proceeded. This miming proved useful later when I took singing lessons.

****

While watching my mother making a cap for Grandma, I asked "Can I make one, Mama?" and she gave me some narrow white lace left over from trimming a petticoat and showed me how to reeve it, make a rosette and she even gave me some scraps of baby ribbon and, lo and behold, I had made a doll's cap or perhaps a hat. Now I knew what I wanted to be when I grew up: a milliner. I begged an empty cardboard box that had held Woodbine packets and by fixing the lid attached to the base to stand up, I had my shop-window. Pins stuck here and there in the bottom of the box made beautiful hat-stands. Searching through the sewing-bag for pieces of pretty material I soon made a stock of hats for my miniature shop. When I showed it to Grandma, all she said was

"Don't worry, Hannah fach, about what you'd like to do when you grow up. You won't have to earn your living when we get the 'stat' back." My father looked pityingly at her whenever she mentioned the 'stat' as he was convinced that there was no hope of getting it. Her faith was unshaken though, and washed over my childhood like a benediction.

Like many Welsh people, Grandma was a staunch Liberal. My father was an incorrigible tease and loved to see her in a temper. I once heard them arguing about a Welsh lawyer, a Baptist of course, who she vowed would become Prime Minister one day. His name was David Lloyd George. Then realising my father was only teasing her she would smile and peace was restored between them.

****

Shirley's mother was very kind under her sharp manner. She gave me my first taste of coconut-cake. I had never tasted anything so delicious and went home demanding that Lizzie make some for us, but Grandma said "Certainly not: it's very indigestible."

It was at Shirley's home, too, that I was given a spoonful of condensed milk. We never had this at home. Knowing a request would meet with the same refusal I suggested to Dick that we buy a small tin to eat upstairs. Sitting on Grandma's bed we ate spoonful after spoonful and threw the tin away, feeling we had tasted 'the food of the gods!' In our haste to finish before we were caught I spilled some on my navy-blue gym-tunic though I didn't realise it at the time. On the following Saturday morning I was taken aback to see my mother looking suspiciously at my tunic which she was ironing in readiness for school on Monday. She and Grandma were wondering why the candle-grease stains wouldn't come out. The hot iron over brown paper which should have melted the grease hadn't succeeded.

"You are big enough now, Doris, not to tip your candle going upstairs to bed. Look at all these grease marks! They won't come out."

I daren't tell them the truth and I had a new tunic.

MY MOTHER

The face of the long-dead is blurred
by the smudging finger of today;
save when a fallen autumn leaf
evokes my mother's auburn hair:
or rain on blackberries portray
her shining, tear-held eyes in grief,
or when a gentle, lilting voice is heard,
then, suddenly, she's there.

HAIKU - Landore, Swansea

The world's metal pulse
limped to Death's halt in Landore;
wealth's slow slide to slag.

In the kitchen, the bookcase with its thirteen panes of glass in each door, was where Grandma hid or thought she hid the sweets she kept for bribing us to take medicine such as senna tea for constipation. When one of the lower panes got broken, I found that by poking a finger through the hole I could just manage to reach the sweets. Dick and I did well out of this, but Grandma soon found her supply diminishing too rapidly and had the pane mended. She had another bribe, though; a threepenny-bit which she would hold in one hand, the cup of horrid senna tea in the other.

The kitchen dresser was full of patterned jugs and dishes and, in my fantasies, became my class of school children, as I was now going to be a teacher. The walking stick my father had cut down for me when I had scalded my leg served as a 'pointer' to the jugs, to which I gave names

"Nellie Greenband, say your two-times table,"or

"Violet Jones, recite 'Helpu Mam',"(Helping mother or

"Don't fidget, Gladys."

Grandma liked the idea of my becoming a teacher. It was so respectable: much better than playing the piano in the 'Pictures', an ambition which I had confided to her.

****

Dr. Gomer Lewis, the minister of the Welsh Baptist Chapel in Swansea, sometimes called to see Grandma. He walked from the front door, straight along the passage leading to the back entrance to the kitchen and had tea with us. One day, when Evelyn was laying tea she remarked that there was a tiny hole in the tablecloth.

"Never mind, Evelyn fach,"said Grandma. "The cloth is clean and paid for and there's only us for tea." But she was wrong. In walked Dr. Gomer Lewis, much to our discomfort. Calmly placing a jam-dish over the hole, Grandma invited him to sit down and join us, her eyes daring us to pick up that dish. Ever afterwards, any tablecloth that had a hole in it was called 'Dr. Gomer Lewis's cloth'.

Customers had seen the reverend gentleman entering the inn and sniggered,

"Look who's slipping into the pub for a crafty drink!"

Everyone in Swansea knew this popular preacher and it was always for tea that he visited us. Had he asked for anything alcoholic , Grandma would have given him a lecture on the evils of strong drink, quoting from the huge black bible always at hand. This bible caused much embarrassment to my sister when she brought home a new boy-friend. The first thing Grandma said to him was "What chapel do you go to?" and woe betide him if he wasn't a Baptist. A Church of England member was beyond the pale.

"Look in your bible my boy and you'll find no mention of christening there" and she opened the bible and read the passage describing the baptism of Christ in the River Jordan.

My friend Eira attended the Congregational Church where the minister, Mr. Thomas, was a saintly-looking man with a long beard. We both thought he was Jesus Christ. He was so like the pictures in my 'Stories from the Bible'. Our own minister was the old-fashioned type of preacher whose voice rose into the kind of chanting we call 'Hwyl' in Wales. Eira and I had arguments about this. She said he sounded as if he were selling coal on the road.

"Grandma, is Mr. Thomas, New Siloh, really Jesus Christ?"

"Certainly not. Mr. Thomas is Congregational and Jesus

Christ was a Baptist," was her indignant reply, which didn't quite satisfy me.

The sermons in our chapel were long and, to young girls, tedious. Evelyn and my cousin Ray, of about the same age, used to cut out a page of funny stories called 'Spare Moments' in my father's weekly paper. They passed it round to their friends to read during the sermon.

"Have you learnt your verse?" was the inevitable question asked every week in Philadelphia Chapel Sunday School. Grandma listened while I recited mine, in Welsh of course. I dreaded doing this and usually hid behind a convenient pillar.

CHAPTER SIX

There was great excitement in our street when two sets of swings were placed at either end of the bare patch which ran between the road and the railway embankment facing The Station Inn. The local children would be able to play here in safety as railings sealed the new playground from the roadway. The first night, the women living in the street themselves took to the swings with wild enthusiasm, going higher and higher for at least an hour. Some of them even stood on the seats. Goodness knows what release of frustration they found in this, but none of us children stood a chance of a ride that night. When Grandma heard about the women's behaviour she was disgusted and didn't encourage us to use the playground, which was a dismal place anyway; no trees, no flowers, just six swings on about forty yards of bare earth.

Dick gave us a fright the day he climbed the railings and slipped, one of thc spikes stabbing his side. When I saw one of our customers carrying him home, pale and dripping blood, I was so stunned I couldn't do anything until I heard a neighbour say "Just look at her. She isn't crying and her little brother all hurt and bleeding!"

I rushed indoors and cried and cried although the doctor told me he would be all right. I sobbed the reason for my tears as Grandma held me close and her reaction was "What can you expect from a woman who rides on the swings put there for children. Come you, Hannah fach."

****

How my mother found time to do all the sewing she did, not only for Evelyn, Dick and myself, but also for my cousins Ray and Gwen, I never knew. I can see now the yards and yards of Welsh flannel for my father's shirts and underpants, which later I heard referred to as "drawers". The shirts were of thick cream flannel with double yokes which yellowed after much washing; the underpants of cream with a narrow black stripe spaced an inch apart. He suffered from asthma and flannel protected his chest.

One morning when I was about seven I was late leaving for school and forgot to take off the 'pinny' I had to wear while eating my breakfast. In class I was ashamed to look up all the morning as my pinny had egg stains on it and discipline was so strict I was afraid to take the pinny off.

For losing my handkerchief every day I got many a telling off and, fed up with this, I said one morning:

"Mama, will you make me a navy blue dress with little white flowers all over it and a frill across here," pointing to my chest a few inches below the neckline.

"Navy blue indeed! Whatever for?" Then Grandma broke in sharply:

"And what's wrong with the pretty dresses your mother makes for you, Madam, and a clean one every day?"

"Because then I can wipe my nose on the frill, like some girls in my class do," I explained, "and then I wouldn't keep losing my hankies all the time." They looked at each other with disgust written all over their faces.

"Right," said my mother, "In future I'll pin your hankies to your dress," adding as she noticed my gloomy face "not a big pin, just a tiny gold one."

So I didn't lose any more handkerchiefs.

One of my classmates was moved up to a higher class, being older than I was, but we still played together in the playground.

"Lend me your hanky," she said one morning during playtime.

"What for?", I asked suspiciously as I unpinned the hanky, hoping she wasn't going to blow her nose in it.

"Only for a lend, that's all. You'll have it back at home-time. I want to take it round the classes to ask who's lost it and I'll come to your class last of all. And by then that old Jography lesson will be over. I hate that old Miss Parsnips."

"Her name is Miss Parsons," I said handing over my hanky, "And mind you give it back to me at home-time." She couldn't try this dodge on more than once but it did help her to skip a hated lesson.

****

Our kitchen was crowded with furniture. There was the big deal table where Evelyn had me sit while she taught me how to tell the time when I was six. It faced the grandfather clock of light oak which I took for granted until the day I saw the one in Shirley's kitchen, which had a painting of the sea above the dial and a ship that tocked back and forth with each tick-tock, magically it seemed.

****

We were very excited in school when a little American girl arrived. She was very striking, with dark hair in long plaits tied with tartan ribbon and wearing a tartan dress. All the children wanted to play with her as they loved to hear her quaint American accent. We called her Yankee May and I was pleased that she was distantly related to my father. She wore a gold ring which I very much envied and I thought she must be rich. To be counted rich you had to have a silk dress, a glass door inside the front door, and a piano. We didn't have a glass door, but I did have a silk dress, a piano, and all the ginger pop I wanted, for nothing, so I was considered rich. Grandma did not approve of Yankee May's ring, though her prejudice was somewhat overcome by my new friend's dainty manner when eating 'cookies' - Chelsea buns. The only way I could eat them was by unwinding the coil of pastry and smothering the length of it with jam after taking out all the currants. The mess on my plate displeased Grandma.

"If you don't like Chelsea buns, Hannah, don't touch them. Look at the state of your plate, and the tablecloth."

"Well, I do like them like this but not the way they are."

I irritated Grandma in other things regarding food. I wouldn't eat the green leaves of cabbage, preferring the hard white stalk. I did not like her tarts, which were brown and crisp on top but lardy and uncooked underneath. They really made me feel sick and the only way I could face eating them was by scraping the fruit from inside and hiding the pastry in my hanky until the meal was over. Then it was slipped into the bowl of bread kept for the chickens. It was only when we had fruit tart, especially blackberry tart, baked on the bakestone on top of the kitchen fire that I could eat every bit, as it was thoroughly cooked that way.

Grandma was not very fond of sweets and that was why Dick and I were always eager to offer her some of ours as we knew she would refuse them: but it gave us a generous feeling. On the other hand, Grandma Matthews was terribly fond of sweets, which we learned to our cost. Realising that she would take two or three from the bag when offered a sweet I thought up a clever idea. I placed one sweet at the top of the bag and, squeezing the bag above the rest, I innocently offered her a sweet. This way she could only get at the one sweet: this amused her so much she never stopped telling the family about my trick, and teasing me.

Grandma bought a tiny wooden stool for Dick. This was for him to hammer tintacks in with his little hammer. He had seen the cobbler do this and it became his favourite hobby. When she saw him put several tintacks in his mouth she was horrified. He said the cobbler did this when mending shoes but promised not to do so again and his hammering continued happily. My father said he inherited this love of handling wood from Grandma Matthews's father, who was a carpenter and undertaker as had been his father before him. Dick's little stool was so covered with tintacks that there was barely a quarter of an inch between them. All over the top, down the sides and all over the legs even. It looked like a headless, tailless steel animal. But when Grandma bought him a brand new stool, thinking he would be thrilled and eager to start covering that with tintacks, he wouldn't touch it and much preferred squeezing tacks in any tiny space on the old stool. So Grandma found a tough piece of material to cover the very new look of the discarded stool and my father asked for Dick's help in tacking it over the top. He was happy to do this and the new stool became a handy little seat for him near the fire.

Dick hadn't always been called Dick. His name was Albert Richard and my mother always called him Bertie, and this she continued to call him long after we decided to call him Dick. In fact, when he was seventeen and had started work at a bank where he had to stay in lodgings, coming home once every three weeks, there were always two letters together from him, one for the family signed 'Dick' and a private one for my mother signed 'Bert'.

During childhood while we were still calling him Bertie we were playing in The Station Inn yard one Saturday morning when Grandma Matthews stopped on her way into the house.

"Catch it, Bertie," someone shouted, throwing a ball towards him, and Grandma whispered to me:

"Don't call him Bertie, Hannah fach. Call him Dick after my lovely brother Dick." I thought it a good idea, but habit dies hard.

Soon after this, my teacher asked which of us in class had a brother named Bertie, at which there was a lot of tittering. I hesitated before putting my hand up, wondering if Dick had fallen down in the playground, when another girl put up her hand and said her brother was Bertie Morris. I was so relieved and decided that Dick was a much nicer name than Bertie, which sounded silly, and that settled it.

Evelyn was named Rachel Evelyn after Grandma Daniel, she being the eldest of us children, and I Hannah Doris after Grandma Matthews. Most children were given biblical names followed by a modern one. Ethel was called Ethel Persis, the latter a biblical name, but Claudia was Claudia Cometa, a name made up from Halley's Comet which had appeared when she was born.

****

Eira's mother went to chapel regularly and I loved to hear her talk about her childhood. She remembered the story of her grandmother, Lisa, who lived in a cottage by the River Tawe in Landore. Lisa used to watch for the boats from France coming up the river for oil. Standing beside a bollard on the bank, a child of six, Lisa was greeted heartily by the Frenchmen who, after leaping ashore, handed her the loop of the tow-rope. With their help she slipped it over the bollard and was rewarded with sixpence. Eagerly waiting for the cargo to be shipped safely, she put her little hands on the loop and again the men helped her to remove it, for which she was paid another sixpence. Eira and I thought she must have become very rich. Imagine how many bars of 'Five Boys' chocolate or how many 'Uncle Luke' sweets you could buy for a shilling!

Every time we walked along Neath Road we would look for that bollard, which was and still is there: though the cottage was derelict I could picture the little girl by the river's edge, placing the rope on the bollard.

It was said that the men working in the oilworks had lovely soft hands because they used to wash them in the oil before leaving work.

****

At The Station Inn no work was allowed to be done on a Sunday that could be done on a Saturday. Potatoes had to be peeled, or 'cleaned' as Grandma would say, and placed in water in the foodsafe. For the Sabbath all signs of 'publicness' had to disappear and the inn became fully a home and very private. Friends who visited were relations, neighbours and chapel-members, though there was little time for either Grandma or my mother to do much entertaining.

Sunday papers were tolerated by Grandma but not read. The only newspapers she read were the Liberal daily called "The Cambria Daily Leader" and the weekly 'Seren Cymru' (Star of Wales), a Baptist publication of course, in which the poems of my grandfather's nephew occasionally appeared. He was what my father described as a 'master of the englyn', a very difficult form of poetry to compose.

When I was caught cutting my nails one Sunday, Grandma said:

"Cut your nails on a Sunday, your safety seek;
The devil will have you the rest of the week."

It was no wonder Dick and I grew bored and, as Grandma said 'Satan finds work for idle hands'. We found naughty things to do such as making toffee when the brown sugar was in short supply or drinking lemonade from the bar when the supply was low.

For all the medicines and buttermilk Grandma gave me, I was still thin, pale and with a deep 'salt-cellar' in my throat. Day after day I would dash up to the bedroom and look eagerly in the mirror to see if it had filled up. But no! I was still a thin, washed-out little thing. One day I found a piece of muslin left over from some curtaining and tried my hand at making a blouse, having watched my mother make one each for Ray, Gwen and Evelyn. It was an easy pattern to copy and soon I was sewing away happily, being careful to make a high neck so as to hide the hated salt-cellar. Proudly I put it on and showed it to the family. They thought it a good try but comical in effect, fitting so badly. When Grandma heard the reason for it all she said we would go to see Miss Woods in Edwards' Department Store in

Swansea and buy a really nice high-necked blouse. My effort ended up in the duster drawer in the dresser.

CHAPTER SEVEN

It was after supper on Sunday evenings that my mother found the only time to indulge in her hobby, Macrame-work. There were balls of cord which she patiently knotted together in some ingenious fashion and the result was a wide fringed band intended to be fixed along the mantel-piece in the parlour, to hang down gracefully.

"Clear the table, Evelyn, and you, John, fetch down the documents." This command was issued from time to time. I looked forward to these sessions, with Grandma giving orders. Throwing my mother a despairing glance, my father reached up to the top of the dresser for the precious box containing the documents relating to the Estate. They were spread on the table.

"Read the list of properties that should come to me," said Grandma. Reciting from the faded yellow pages Evelyn gave the names of farms in Carmarthenshire, and their acreage.

"Now read William's property," and another longer list was read out. Though I helped my mother with her Macrame-work I found the idea of our inheriting all this property much more interesting, especially the castle connected with the estate.

"Why should he have more than you?" I asked Grandma.

"Because he was a man and older than me," was the reply.

But of all the papers, what excited me most was a letter that had been found in 'Plas Newydd', Grandma's home in Llanedi. It lay in a bureau and had come from the family solicitor, written to Grandma's great-uncle urging him to claim the estate now in Chancery. I can see my mother now, painstakingly twisting the cord in her Macrame-work, as she listened to Evelyn reading.

"This is a copy of an old letter found in a bureau belonging to the late Richard Seys Pryce - bachelor, brother of Francis Pryce of Plas Newydd, Llanedi. Found in the year 1895."

Cowbridge,
June 10, 1834.

My dear Sir,

This is to inform you that there is an heir wanted to enjoy the estate of Boverton in Glamorgan, otherwise known as Treberedd.

Dear sir, Why don't you try for it. I know very well that you are the rightful heir to it by your late grandfather, Mr. Francis Lewis Pryce of Erwastad, Llanedi, who married Mrs. Seys of Boverton widow of Evan Seys Esq. Boverton Castle. She had no issue by the Evan Seys aforesaid, but she had four children by your grandfather of Erwastad in the parish of Llanedi in the county of Carmarthen, namely Richard Pryce, your uncle, Francis Pryce, your father, Elizabeth and Jane Pryce, your two aunts. Your uncle and two aunts had an annuity from the Boverton Castle for life. Mrs. Pryce buried your grandfather Francis Lewis Pryce, then married Mr. Blades of Bath. She had no children by him. She buried him. She then married a Mr. Briscoe, a gentleman in the army. She had no children by him. She outlived the four husbands. She had no children but by your grandfather Francis Lewis Pryce."

Evelyn paused. Grandma gave us all an expressive look which said "Now can't you see why I believe the estate will come to the family one day?"

My father had gone into the bar for some tobacco. He had heard all this so many times before and took a realistic view of things. My mother was engrossed in her Macrame-work. I think that I alone of all the grandchildren sitting at the table was thrilled with what I heard. I fell to thinking, 'Fancy Grandma's great-great grandmother lived in a castle. How romantic! Then why are we living in an inn? Only Grandma and I were alive to the prospect.

My cousin Ray suggested another cup of tea. Ray's name was really Rachel. Addressing Evelyn, Grandma commanded "Go on, bach" and Evelyn resumed reading from the letter:

"After a while, she left Boverton and went to live at Hotwells, Bath. Then she died and was buried at Boverton Castle, Glamorganshire. Some of the children are living now but are very old.

Some years ago, your brother Francis Lewis Pryce, of 'Plas Newydd', Llanedi, gave a copy of your grandmother's will."

Here Evelyn paused again: she couldn't understand the faded handwriting, and passed over the next few words, picking up the narrative again when the writer said

"and the counsel's opinion which was in favour of the Seys, namely your grandfather."

Then followed names of people who had tried to claim the Estate and of those who had bought parts of the Estate in spite of the fact that "no good title" could be produced. The Estate was then thrown "into Chancery". Evelyn was tired of reading but Grandma insisted on her finishing the letter, which delighted me with its old-fashioned language.

"I had a talk with your brother, Mr. Francis Pryce, about the concern of Boverton and he said to me that no one had the greater right to the property than you by your grandfather's will. There are now £100,000 in the Lord Chancellor's hands, rent-duty from the estate and will soon be doubled if not claimed. When your grandmother had the estate, they received £2,500 from them. I suppose you know where the estate lies. Boverton Castle is four miles from Cowbridge and six miles from Cardiff.

Sir, I wish you would make all convenient speed to go to the Registrar"; (Here Evelyn faltered again over the faded writing) "of Llandaff, and get a copy of your grandmother's will. Then immediately to London and wait on the Lord Chancellor. When you arrive there please to call first on my nephew, John Williams, a solicitor of Gray's Inn, and mention the case to him and he will go with you to the Lord Chancellor who will see that you have justice done to you, for I am sure that you are the right and only heir to the estate of Boverton. I stated the case to my nephew, all about the matter, some time ago and he told me that it is your right to try for it.

Please to write to me and let me know how it goes on, in which I wish you all the good luck and happiness in this old world and, in the world to come, everlasting life.

I remain, dear Sir, ever your well-wisher,

Your most obedient servant,

Geo. Williams, (late clerk to your dear old father)."

"Funny way to spell Joe," remarked Evelyn, "G.E.O."

"Its not Joe," said Grandma, "it's short for 'George'."

My father returned from the bar where he had been filling his tobacco pouch and said wearily, "It's no good, you know. It will mean engaging a barrister to read the documents and will cost the earth. As I've told you time and time again it's the hardest thing in the world to get anything out of Chancery."

Grandma glared at him, but he continued "Anyway it's not you would benefit if you did win the case, nor your brother William's oldest son. It says something about 'male heirs forever', doesn't it?".

"I'm quite aware of that, John." (She was the only one who called him John. My mother called him Jack) "I want my brother William's children to have what's their right, by my great-great grandmother's will."

When Evelyn had put all the papers back in the box, Grandma slammed down the lid, snapping "And don't tell me about my family's affairs." We drank our tea in silence. I felt angry and hurt.

I never tired of hearing about the Estate and hoped my father would find out more about it, but whatever was said he invariably remarked "That may not be true."

"But it says in this book" Grandma responded triumphantly, "that King John fled to Boverton Castle to escape the barons." She paused for effect, "And I'll tell you why. Because it was there that his former wife was living."

"They wouldn't dream of looking for him there. That would be the last place, wouldn't it?" I said eagerly.

"You shouldn't believe all you read in books" my father retorted. "Anyway, that's nothing to do with your family and a right to the Boverton estate."

"And it says too" continued Grandma, "that there is still a room in the castle they call 'King John's Hole', where he hid."

It made me mad when my father put a damper on all that Grandma so stubbornly believed. I wished so much that our family story should have a happy ending. My young life would have been sadly lacking in romance without the talk about the Estate. Sunday evenings with the important box on the table and its faded documents being read aloud, slowly, were precious to me.

Looking at her I felt, 'Surely Grandma would grace a castle with her dignified manner!'

I never took to the odd little woman who called from time to time to see Grandma, never staying very long and taking no notice of anyone else. A stout figure, upholstered in black, she was I gathered on her way to see some bishop or other in Cardiff, who held important documents concerning the Estate. I pricked up my inquisitive ears at the mention of the Estate, but as they whispered in Welsh I didn't understand much of what was said. She carried a huge black leather bag containing, I imagined, more documents and I saw that she had no welcome from my father, who watched the gold sovereigns being handed to her. I saw Grandma put her hand into her pocket, low down in the folds of her long black skirt and bring out her purse: not a purse as we know it, but a leather pouch with a metal ring round the top. I can see Grandma now, slipping the shining coins from the pouch into her left hand, then into the eager, grasping hand of the woman, a person distrusted by my father, disliked by my mother, but welcomed and wholly trusted by Grandma as a worker on the family's behalf towards regaining the Estate. When my father tried to reason with her, she wouldn't hear a word against her visitor, saying that relations, even some in America, had sent money which would be spent on engaging a barrister to claim the Estate.

"Can't you see there are others with a stronger claim?" my father asked insistently. "Look at the Seys family: they have tried and they've lost to Chancery, so what sense is there in your throwing away money like that?"

"It's according to my ancestor's will, so there!"

It was no use arguing any further, so he gave up trying.

Grandma's final words were, "Remember, John, she was Elizabeth Seys, her father being Richard Seys of Boverton Castle. She married her cousin Evan Seys, but they had no children. It was after she married my great-great grandfather, Lewis Pryce, that she had children, and that's where our claim stands. I know what I'm talking about, thank you."

At these signs of temper my mother motioned my father to stop, and Grandma's faith remained unshaken.

My little body would stiffen with pride as Grandma read from a history book that the wife of So and So ("One of our family, remember") was "At the court of Queen Elizabeth the First, and that's a long, long time ago, mind you."

All the legal jargon of 'entailed estate' and 'male heirs for ever' was bewildering and not convincing to my mind.

"Was Boverton Castle haunted?" I asked.

"Give the child the book to read for herself" demanded Grandma, and eagerly I read.

"Some men who were taking down a part of the building said they had seen in the twilight the figure of a woman dressed in mourning clothes of an ancient fashion. Her hair hung down her back and her face was covered. The apparition moved from room to room of the building very slowly and sometimes the silence of the place was broken by her sobs. One of the workmen was telling an old inhabitant about it and he remarked:

'Oh, that was Wissey, the King's widow. I've often seen her.' This refers to Isabella, called Hadwisa, who married King John, and was divorced on the pretext that there were no children of the marriage. She retired to Boverton."

So there *was* a ghost and that was thrilling, but frightening too.

My father took the book away from me but I made up my mind that one day I would go to Boverton and, if I was brave enough, stay until night so that I might see the ghost of 'Wissey', which I thought a pretty little pet name. Fancy an ex-queen having a pet name, just like ordinary people!

****

"Tell me about when you were a little girl, Mama." She was busy ironing and I sat at the kitchen table watching her as she paused to spit on the iron, freshly-heated on the red-hot coal fire. Then she held the iron near her cheek to see if it was hot enough, but not too hot to iron the chemise belonging to one of the girls, Evelyn, Gwen and Ray.

"Well, when your Auntie Sally and I were small, we lived at The Kingsbridge Inn as you know. It wasn't only an inn at that time; part of it was a grocer's shop." She put the iron down and folded the chemise and added it to the pile of ironing.

"I remember one hot summer day. Grandma was topping gooseberries in the kitchen and had taken off her shoes to put her feet on the cool flagstones, when she heard a tiny noise in the shop."

Clapping my hand to my mouth in excitement, expecting to hear something thrilling, I asked "What did Grandma do?"

"She crept in her stockinged feet into the shop and there, with her hand in the money drawer, was a gipsy."

"Wasn't she afraid?"

"No. Your grandmother gripped the woman's dirty wrist and made her drop the money, which rolled on the counter and then she pushed her out of the shop and shut the door."

"Wasn't she a little bit frightened of the gipsy?" I asked again, my eyes big with imagined fright.

"No, she was a brave woman, your Grandma, really brave." Placing the iron on the heavy triangular iron-stand, my mother resumed thoughtfully:

"When I was a very little girl in Kingsbridge, there was an outbreak of cholera in Wales. People were dying like flies everywhere and an old lady living near us had cholera, and no one would go near her house. They were terrified of catching the dreadful disease."

"I expect Grandma went though," I said confidently.

"Yes, she did, and she tended the old woman until she died, but Grandma didn't have the cholera. Several of those who refused to help did." My mother's eyes were dreamy.

"Do you know, Hannah fach, when I was ten I used to do all the accounts in the grocery part. I was a good scholar, Grandma used to say." And she finished the ironing.

CHAPTER EIGHT

On our way to school we had to pass along a row of houses that had no pavement, but each house had a big, square flag-stone in front of the doorstep. Every morning as we came by a woman would be scrubbing her flag-stone and it was tempting for us to jump on these stones as we ran along to school. Invariably the woman rushed out shouting after us for soiling her clean stone. Her daughter, Mabel, was in my class and when I learned that the woman was her stepmother I accepted the fact, convinced that it was because she was always scrubbing the stone on which we stepped. Eira, too, believed this and when I told Grandma about it she laughed and explained.

"I remember when Mabel's mother was married in our chapel. Poor girl, she died soon afterwards leaving a baby girl. The father married again. That's why Mabel has a stepmother instead of a real mother. Scrubbing the step indeed!"

****

Although shops weren't open legally on Sundays, there was a house nearby where the woman made ginger pop. This was a white, cloudy drink you could buy for twopence for a pint and a half bottle. Beer cost twopence a pint: the best quality threepence. We had plenty of lemonade in the bar but it was a change to have something bought somewhere else.

****

Dick was a very tender-hearted little boy and when his kitten died we had to have a proper funeral. The empty wooden cigar-box my father found for us for a coffin was too shallow, and as we closed the lid Dick began to cry saying it was hurting poor little Blackie. Grandma then suggested an empty Woodbine box would be kinder as it was made of cardboard and would bend. This worked well and we went to the backyard to find a nice spot for a grave. There was an unused stable where coal was kept, and alongside it a grassy patch, well away from the path leading from the back door of the inn to the gate to the next street. Here we sadly buried Blackie but soon forgot him when we were given another little kitten.

Dick loved small animals and when any of the neighbours had a new baby my mother simply had to take Dick to see it. He loved babies, and even when a grown boy in the Big Boy's School, if he met anyone he knew nursing a baby he would stop to admire and talk to the baby. It didn't matter that his friends were quite embarrassed. My father could talk baby talk for hours, long after my mother had exhausted her conversation. I think Dick inherited this lovable trait from my father and from Grandma Matthews, who adored all children.

****

While my father did his 'books' on Sunday afternoons Grandma and my mother went to bed for a nap. When we came home from Sunday School Dick and I had to wait for our tea, which meant naughty work for our idle hands. We found, among a pile of washing in the Brewhouse a pair of Grandma's stays, out of which stuck a thin, flat piece of metal stiffening she called a 'steel'. It was just the thing to make a make-believe cut-throat razor. Having watched my father shaving we got a bowl of soapy water and lathered our faces, taking it in turn to shave each other with the steel. It was fun, so we decided to soap our faces again and were ready to begin when Grandma appeared, to see two pairs of eyes in faces covered in lather.

At that time my hair was brushed straight back and tied with a bow of ribbon on top of my head, the curly hair hanging down my back. It was on another such Sunday afternoon of boredom on returning from Sunday School that we found my mother's sharp sewing scissors. Looking in the kitchen mirror I pushed them right up through the front of my hair and cut off a huge clump, leaving a brush standing up. Dick watched helplessly, knowing there would be an awful row. I tried several ways of hiding the grotesque bush and in the end found that by combing the side pieces over the front it would be hidden, if not for long. Of course, there was a terrible row and, though Grandma tried curling it the hairs were too short to be gripped properly in the curling papers. We had to wait until it grew. It did, but not before the school photographer came to school and there it was for all to see. While we were in the line waiting for the exciting-looking black cloth to be fixed over his head, my teacher called out:

"Keep your head up straight, Doris Matthews. It's all to one side."

I obeyed but by the time the man was ready, there I stood, with my head bent sideways as usual and that hideous brush sticking up in front of my hair. Whenever I was able to slip up to the bedroom I tried combing the side hair over the front, but each time I was caught, and Grandma pulled it back to reveal the spiky result: a lesson I suppose to punish me for chopping my hair. Grandma told me that young ladies used to pile their hair up in front and that one evening in chapel an embarrassing thing happened. A girl sitting in the front row of the gallery bowed her head in prayer, her hat perched on top of her puffed-up hair, when suddenly her hat fell back and her front hair unfolded, covering her face. But at the same moment a rolled-up stocking fell on the lap of a surprised gentleman sitting downstairs. She had used the stocking to make her hair look abundant.

Of course I dreaded having to take a message to Grandma Matthews during that endless period of waiting for my hair to grow back, as she teased me unmercifully.

Although it was Grandma who curled my hair, Evelyn's was curled by my mother in an utterly different way. Her hair was long and very dark and straight. Long strips of white sheeting were used, about an inch and a half wide. The hair was divided into eight or ten tresses: the curling started at the top of the hair, Evelyn holding one strip-end tightly against her head, while my mother wound the tress round and round the strip like a firm bandage, to the last inch of hair. Then the strip of linen was wound round and round up to the top of the tress, where the ends were tied together. The result looked like candles hanging from her head and were most uncomfortable.

Many girls in my class had their hair curled in this way and on one occasion, when there was to be a school concert in the evening, several girls came to school with these curlers still in their hair. The teacher was very cross and told them to 'take off those white rags' before coming to school in the afternoon. The curls didn't look as natural as those Grandma made and I longed for my hair to grow long enough to be curled, but though Grandma did her best, she failed.

I was going to a friend's birthday party one Saturday and as usual Grandma had curled my hair. What did I find when I woke up but my hair straight and all my curlers on the dressing table! I must have dreamed I was getting ready for the party and got up during the night, taken the curlers out and gone back to bed. Ray produced a pair of curling tongs she sometimes used and, sticking these in the fire, managed to twist my hair into curls, or rather frizzes, which were better than nothing.

How I envied Eira's black, curly hair while she envied me my long, fair, straight hair. As we sat outside her front door eating a bar of Cadbury's chocolate, a woman passing by remarked "You look like 'Night and Day'," which thrilled us. It sounded complimentary to Eira's dark brown eyes and hair and my fairness.

If I felt thirsty during an evening in the week, and had my hair done up in those comical, bun-shaped, agonising curlers, with their stiff brownpaper ends twisted and sticking out all round my head, it was embarrassing to have to go through the middle kitchen to the filter in the bar. This was an enormous brown stone jar with a tap, which was cleaned out every Sunday morning for fresh charcoal to be placed in as a filter. Water from this was the only water we were allowed to drink.

Once, when I was offered in a friend's house, a cup of water from a tap, I was quite sure I would be poisoned and I did not like the idea of drinking from a cup as I was used to a glass, so I hesitated, but risking my life, I drank it. I didn't die, so I tried filling a cup of water from the tap in the brewhouse and was about to drink it, though feeling guilty, when Grandma came in. She was very cross.

"What next?" she exclaimed. "If you want a drink of water fetch some from the filter. A cup of water from the tap, if you please'."

You couldn't argue with Grandma. I didn't try to explain that I had found it was all right to drink water from a tap and that a cup was as good as a glass. Seeing my crestfallen face she said "Come on, Hannah fach, I'll fetch you some 'pop'."

****

When Grandma and I were in bed she "cwtched" (cuddled) me. This I loved, except that sometimes she would suddenly moan and leap out of bed.

"It's only the cramp, Hannah fach: go you to sleep."

By now she was standing on the patch of linoleum in front of the window, where she remained for a while. Sure enough the cramp had gone and she was back in bed cuddling me again. That linoleum surely had some magic in it, I thought.

The one day of the year when I wished I didn't have to sleep with Grandma was Christmas Eve. I woke when it was still dark, longing to get at my mother's black stocking hanging at the foot of the brass bedstead, to see what Daddy Christmas had brought me. We always said Daddy Christmas, not Father Christmas or Santa Claus.

"Go to sleep, child," Grandma said as I wriggled, but how could I when I was so excited? Sometimes I managed to slip down as far as possible by dragging myself against the wall and grabbing the stocking and lifting it over the bedclothes. Even in the dark I knew the big round lumps were an orange and an apple, the small lumps nuts, but I couldn't guess what the bulky parcels might be. Still, there was always a doll sticking its head out of the top of the stocking. It seemed hours before it was light enough to creep out of bed and to stand by the window holding the presents up to see what they were before running into Dick's bedroom to show them and to see his.

When the day came that we were told the disappointing truth about Daddy Christmas, Dick and I were so broken-hearted that we planned to act Daddy Christmas to each other, telling no one. We bought each other small gifts but somehow these only half-filled the stockings and when Grandma took us on Christmas morning into the middle kitchen to have our presents which were arranged on the settle by the fire, our eyes were full of disillusionment. The miniature sweet-shop and colouring books weren't nearly as enchanting as if they had come from Daddy Christmas. I had a big lump in my throat and I think Dick did too, but I choked it back by suggesting that we go next door to see what the children there thought of the presents we had bought them.

For weeks we had saved for the important day when we would go to Swansea shopping for our Christmas gifts for our neighbours' children. There was only one place for this, The Penny Bazaar. This was a long, open stall in the arcade off Goat Street. Here were arrayed hundreds of lovely things you could buy, all at a penny each. We bought carefully for each child, choosing what we knew they would like: pencils, crayons and crayoning books, crudely-cut Japanese dolls which could easily be clothed, and all sorts of games.

****

Every summer there was a procession of Sunday School children from many chapels, representing the Temperance Movement. The adherents, who were parents of these children, did not allow them to play with us even in the inn yard.

I stood watching them as they marched down the street behind the inn and was hurt when one of my friends walked past, ignoring me at the back gate. It was very hot and the children had been out in the sun for a long time. Impulsively I called some of them into our yard for some 'pop', which they were eagerly enjoying when one of the deacons saw them and dragged them away. It was a crime even to go anywhere near strong drink it seemed.

****

When work became scarce in Landore many men went to America to work in the tin-mines. They set off in small groups and, as going as far afield as London was quite an occasion for most of them, going to the vast United States was a great adventure. One of our chapel members was taking this great step and was travelling alone to a job in New York State. When settled there he was to send for his wife and family, along with as many of their possessions as could be dealt with on such a voyage. Families had been known to take feather-beds and household utensils along, as if the Americans had no such amenities.

The evening of departure came at last and I was glad, as it meant giving this lone traveller a big send-off. A crowd of his friends and relations gathered on Landore Station and as soon as he was seated in the train the singing began. A wait of perhaps a quarter of an hour allowed time for rousing choruses, sung with fervour and many tears. The one that was most popular ran,

"How can I bear to leave thee,
One parting kiss I give thee" etc.

The chorus was,

"Farewell, farewell, my own true love,
Farewell, farew-e-ll, my o-w-n true love."

That the words were not very suitable didn't affect the popularity of the song and as the train pulled out he would wave to the crowd, the music following him in the evening air.

****

We had season tickets for the train journey from Landore to Swansea, which was convenient, as The Station Inn was only a few minutes' walk from the station. When Evelyn and I were returning from Swansea one day she was asked to go into the office on the platform as she had committed a serious offence a few days earlier. Evelyn had no idea what she was supposed to have done. Her innocent manner impressed the railway detective, who had accused her of travelling without a ticket and he said he would call and speak to our parents. Grandma was very upset and we were all bewildered as Evelyn had never gone to town by train without having her ticket in her handbag. But someone had, and when questioned, gave Evelyn's name and address, saying she had left her season ticket at home. The girl was cautioned and allowed to continue her journey.

Dick and I were thrilled to hear that a detective was in our parlour, 'investigating a crime' as we thought. We listened outside the parlour door in the passage as the detective described the offender, a plump girl with dark curls, not in the least like my sister. It was Grandma who recognised the girl and my mother and Evelyn went to her house, where she confessed. She said she had caught the train at the last minute and when the inspector asked to see her ticket, in panic, gave Evelyn's name. She thought the inspector would simply check it with the list of season-ticket holders and leave it at that. Her mother was a poor widow, my mother explained, and that was the last we heard of the matter.

****

Our servant, Lizzie, was a treasure and confidante of my childish delights and woes. Although always very busy, she somehow managed to find time for Eira and me when we had problems, so that when she left to get married it was a difficult time for Grandma and my mother. An elderly widow came to clean for us, daily, but when my mother caught her slyly filling a small bottle from a large container in the bar and slipping it into her canvas apron pocket, she had to leave.

Next, Maggie from the Patri (Pottery?) was employed. We liked her on sight, a dumpy, fresh-faced, pleasant girl with a square smile always on her square face, which shone with vigorous washing. Her teeth were white and even but the effect was spoiled by their being so tiny and her gums so prominent. Maggie was always singing as she worked but for some reason her favourite song was "God Save the King". She was homesick away from her large family and once, when I helped her make the beds, she gazed longingly out of the back bedroom window towards her home.

"And there's Nentical Row" she said, pointing to some houses in the distance. "That's where our Sarah Jane is going to live when she gets married."

Maggie had the day off for the wedding. Eira and I longed to hear the details.

"She looked lovely in a white dress and apple-blossom on her head: from the apple-tree in the garden," Maggie said. Among the presents was "a thing made of real silver" we were told "as it says E.P.N.S. on it." I wondered what this could be. Soon after this Evelyn was laying tea and placed a bowl of lump sugar and tongs beside it on the table cloth, when Maggie remarked with surprise, "Is that's what it's for then? On the mankle-piece it is in our Sarah Jane's house. Well, well!"

Maggie was liked by all the customers, but one day she did not return following her afternoon off. Evelyn and I were sent to find her house and take her wages to her. We hoped to see her but her father opened the door, took the money and nodded his thanks. We left without a glimpse of Maggie. On our way home we walked along 'Nentical Row' which turned out, on reading, to be 'Nightingale Row.' We learned soon afterwards that Maggie was married and 'not a day too soon' I heard Grandma say to my mother, who had noticed how plump Maggie had grown when she was pegging out the washing one day.

There were difficulties in getting a replacement, but eventually we found a refined young Englishwoman, Ettie, from a Monmouthshire village. The young men were all after her from the day she started, especially our milkman. I revelled in watching the courtship though my mother was more afraid of losing yet another good servant than in watching a romance. Ettie's father was suddenly taken ill, however, and she left immediately to look after him. I assumed the milkman would be broken hearted but he was seen with another girl quite soon, which I thought heartless and not true love.

There was nothing charming about the next servant, Harriet: a hard-faced woman who liked to say that no man could be trusted, and that every girl who got married in the district did so because she had to. No man would seduce Harriet, never fear!

I heard Grandma tell her, slyly, in Welsh:

"Every fortress is impregnable until it is besieged."

My father translated this deep remark for me into English.

Harriet was a good worker and that was what was needed at The Station Inn.

CHAPTER NINE

Sunday mornings saw men walking sedately down the roads to chapel, always dressed in sober black suits. If they walked with one arm held along the back I was convinced they were deacons. I suppose it was a habit among chapel members, but I thought they had to be deacons before they were allowed to walk in that fashion. There was one outstanding gentleman whom we saw going to our chapel, in gleaming top hat and with shoes shining like new. I was awed to hear that his shoes were polished underneath the soles as well as above, to preserve the leather. No one else seemed to do this. He was a fine musician and when Evelyn began giving piano lessons she visited his house to teach his children. The gentleman was John Hughes, composer of the second national anthem of Wales, 'Calon Lan' (a pure heart), and the chapel indeed the whole town, were very proud of him.

Grandma told me that the words of that famous hymn were written by a bard, 'Gwyrosydd', whom she called the Shakespeare of Wales. He used to call at The Station Inn, an unassuming, shabby working man who, on one occasion called for a drink on his way to an important Eisteddfod in which he was competing. He was wearing a shabby old muffler and Grandpa lent him a collar and tie so that he would look decent in front of all those hundreds of people, where he would surely win a prize and must face everyone when mounting the platform to receive it. Grandma was proud that both men were known to her.

****

In the next class in school, my teacher was very tall and thin. We called her 'Skinny Minnie' and simply waited for the end of the year when we would move up a class where there might be a teacher more like Miss Padden. I had to write a composition about holidays. One poor little girl had hers put aside while the teacher read all the others aloud. Later, the child was given a scolding for writing in her composition:

"Last summer I went on a honeymoon with my big sister." As she told me this in the playground, neither of us could understand why Skinny Minnie had been so cross. To us, going on a honeymoon meant, in our innocence, going on a holiday.

Every teacher had a 'signal' or what we called a 'click'. This was a contraption made of yellow wood. It had a trigger-like piece attached which, when pressed sharply down then released made a clicking noise. It was used in singing lessons to tell us when to start singing, and during lessons if the children made too much noise. We knew we must stop chattering when we heard the 'click'. During my long period of absence from school I tried to make one of these so that I could play 'school', but it didn't work at all. Then something happened that took my mind off playing 'school'.

"Well, well, here's a card from Alf. From Turkey this time." This kind of news never failed to excite me. I'd heard so much about this Uncle Alf, my grandfather Daniel's sister's son, who was a steward at sea, travelling the world and sending wonderful coloured picture postcards to his Aunty Rachel, as he called Grandma. The day he arrived to spend a leave with us was the beginning of my desire to visit the exciting places at which his ship had called. From Turkey he brought me a pair of exquisitely beaded mules in turquoise satin. Mules were uncommon in those days and although they fitted me perfectly they were much too precious to wear. I hung them on a nail on the bedroom wall.

Uncle Alf had the gift of mimicry and when he told a story set in France, spoke in broken English with shrugs and gestures which delighted his hearers. He and I sat on the settle in the kitchen, with a big map of the world spread out on the table, and he would trace his last voyage for me. I was determined that one day I too would travel abroad to see these wonderful places for myself. He seemed to me like a god with a touch of magic.

As a little boy Uncle Alf had spent his school holidays at his Aunty Rachel's house and when at boarding school, which he hated, at the end of one holiday he simply ran away to sea. I was very impressed by all he told me, especially one thing that happened to his half-brother, also a sailor. He had been born with a caul over his face and to a seaman this means that as long as he kept the caul with him he would never suffer death by drowning. Many a captain offered him a lot of money for the caul but he refused to sell it until one voyage when he was short of money. He was drowned on his next voyage. Here again was something magical.

Uncle Alf was very useful in the kitchen.

"Alf can make mutton broth out of water gruel" Grandma said more than once. He would search in the larder for odd bits of cold meat and with vegetables and his own ingenuity concoct a tasty meal to which he gave a French name, like 'ragout'.

"Now here is Constantinople" he said, pointing to the map; and I interrupted him with "I wish I could come with you."

"Why not," he teased, just to get me excited. "You can come with me as a kitchen boy when you are a bit older."

"Did you hear that, Grandma? Uncle can take me with him as a kitchen-boy."

"Kitchen boy did you say? But you are a girl" replied Grandma.

"But you'd have to have all that lovely hair cut off," said Uncle Alf.

"I don't mind, honestly," and he smiled, wickedly, with his twinkling blue eyes.

"Stop it, Alf," Grandma said firmly. "Telling the child such rubbish," her serious brown eyes hardening.

"Of course, you could come as a passenger if you had the money." Frantically I counted my birthday present money, all so pitifully small compared with the deliberately reckoned high cost of such a voyage.

"I know," I said, "I'll have Evelyn's fifty pounds."

"What?" said Grandma in horror.

"Yes, the money Uncle Daniel left her."

Uncle Daniel was Grandfather Daniel's brother, named Daniel Daniel. He visited us occasionally and gave each of us a bar of plain chocolate cream, which none of us liked. He left nothing to Dick or myself in his will, and here was I planning to get hold of Evelyn's money to finance my trip with Uncle Alf, I didn't think of discussing the idea with Evelyn, who would certainly have considered it the height of impudence.

Uncle Alf's shore leaves in Wales were something to look forward to and his postcards showed when he was nearing home. I adored him and it was only recently when looking through some old photographs that I realised he was a tall, handsome man with blue eyes and, as Grandma used to say, 'Cassie's nose'. My mother's name was Catherine but she was called Cassie by the family. To me Uncle Alf was the loving kindly giant whom Grandma continually warned about being too fond of his beer.

"Come on, Alf, give us one of your stories" a customer asked. "Tell us the one about the little negro boy and the missionary." Uncle Alf told with relish and much gesticulation the story, using pidgin English for the little boy and very refined English for the missionary. They were all eager to buy him a drink when he had finished his story, doubly interesting to those who had probably not been further than Cardiff. By eleven o'clock he was often tiddly. This distressed Grandma, who was very fond of him, and her rebukes were always gentle. Yet, in spite of his ability to learn foreign languages, not fluently but enough to make himself understood in foreign ports, Uncle Alf utterly failed to learn Welsh, the language spoken at home. If my parents were talking in Welsh and he came into the room, my mother would say "Oh, Jack. It's very rude of us to talk Welsh in front of Alf as he doesn't understand a word we're saying" and they would continue their conversation in English for his benefit. Because of this, my own knowledge of conversational Welsh was limited. We heard only English in school, except during a Welsh lesson.

It was at the end of one of his leaves and his ship 'The Duchess of Cornwall' was in Swansea Docks. We were all sad that evening as it meant goodbye for goodness knows how many long months before we'd see him again. My mother was very concerned, as everyone wanted to buy 'Good old Alf' a last drink and he had to catch the last tram to Swansea and find his way to his ship. I know I cried a little inside as he left the inn and walked down the street with his slight sailor's roll.

Long after midnight, a heavy knocking at the front door woke us all up and sent my father hurrying into his black and white striped flannel drawers and jacket and down the stairs. There, sheepishly waiting at the door, stood Uncle Alf. He had caught the tram, but on reaching the docks had failed in his fuddled state to locate his ship. So he had walked all the way back to the inn. "The Duchess of Cornwall" went down with all hands and Grandma thanked God that Uncle Alf hadn't been sober enough to catch the ship or he would have been drowned. He gave up going to sea then and lived with us until he died many years later.

Having him live with us was a blessing, as my father's health deteriorated. He suffered so badly from asthma that his breathing sounded like an organ playing and the chest of drawers in his bedroom was covered with bottles of medicine and inhalants. My father had great faith in herbs which were boiled, strained, and when cold, bottled. Grandma saw that he took so many glassfuls a day. One day, a new servant seeing the bowl of what looked like water with grass and leaves in it, threw it down the sink and there was a row about it as it took lengthy preparation.

****

There was one celebration evening we couldn't enjoy at The Station Inn, and that was 'Apple and Candle Night', or Halloween. But a neighbour used to let us join her children in the fun. A bathful of cold water was placed on the kitchen floor with apples bobbing on the water. We had to kneel down with our hands behind our backs, all around the bath and try to catch an apple in our mouths. There was water splashed all over the stone floor, but it was fun. In the parlour a long stick hung from the ceiling with a cross piece attached, swinging just above our eye-level. An apple was stuck on one end of this stick and a lighted candle fixed at the other. Again we had to have our hands placed behind our backs, this time standing, and try to bite the apple, taking care not to get burned by the swinging candle. As we children darted at the apple, the stick swung more and more wildly.

One Saturday morning Eira and I went along with some other children to a small shop kept by 'Jane y Bont' (Jane of the Bridge). It was almost under a bridge and Jane was famous for her 'starvers'. These were large slices of stiff bread pudding containing a few currants. I think they cost a penny each. When I walked into the inn eating my starver, Grandma stared in surprise, as I had never liked bread and butter pudding as she made it with eggs and milk. And here was I, eating a dry lump of bread pudding. But I wasn't sorry when she took it from me and put it in the basin for the chickens.

The bedroom where Grandma and I slept together was at the far end of the clubroom where members of The Foresters Club met once a week. It meant having to walk the length of that long room in my hated curlers, carrying my candle. It was interesting, though, to peep through the tiny bedroom window high up in the door when a lantern lecture was being given, but my toes ached painfully from standing on tip toe to draw aside the flowered muslin curtain covering it. Two steps led down into the bedroom. I loved this idea of stepping down into a room and still do.

The only time I have slept in a four-poster bed was when Grandma took me for a holiday to Llanwrda, a quiet little country village. This was during one of my frequent absences from school through illness. We stayed at the only hotel there, "The Vale of Towy". The kind landlady fussed over me and used to take me down into the cool cellar where huge sides of bacon and ham hung. Slicing a thin piece of lean ham she told me to eat it raw: it would make me strong, she said, and though I ate it every morning I have never wanted to do so since.

I made friends with the only little girl I could find to play with, the station master's daughter Edith, who was a few years older than I was. She took me along to her music lesson, which interested me as I had not yet learned the piano but liked to attempt little tunes by ear on Evelyn's piano at home.

Her teacher, a man, was amused when I said I could play a hymn 'all on the black notes'. He let me play 'O happy day that fixed my choice', but made no comment. I had expected him to be impressed as I thought it very clever to be able to play on the black notes only. I suspect that playing by ear was not considered good musically and Edith played slowly from Hemy's Tutor which I had watched her practising at her home. Neither did her teacher appreciate the fact that I had been teaching her to play 'O happy day' without the music and without using white notes.

I fed the chickens and went on short walks with Grandma, but the quiet of the countryside began to pall and the only story book in the hotel started off with the sentence 'Tom woke up betimes one summer morning', which I didn't understand, though Grandma said it just meant 'before he usually woke'. I thought it promised to be a silly story and left it unread.

When we found that I had run out of clean dresses, I suggested hopefully that we had better go home, but that morning Grandma had received a letter from Claudia saying that in a few days she would be passing through Llanwrda on her way to Llandrindod Wells and asked if we could be on the platform as her train passed through, so that she could wave to us. That might have provided us with some excitement, but Grandma had a better idea. She wrote at once to my mother asking her to pack a parcel of clean dresses for me which Claudia could throw through the window of the compartment as the train went by. So there we waited, Grandma, Edith and I on Llanwrda platform, and sure enough, there was Claudia at the window and the next minute the parcel flopped on the platform quite near where we were standing.

But, new dresses or not, our holiday was cut short because I developed raging toothache, and all Grandma's 'cwtching' in the four-poster with its floral curtaining, couldn't ease the pain. There was nothing for it but an early return to Swansea and a visit to our dentist, Mr. Forbes Scott, whom I wasn't a bit afraid of seeing, as he was so kind and understanding of small girls.

Saturday night was the busiest time of the week at The Station Inn, so we saw little of our parents during the evening. This was when we had our special supper, cooked in the Dutch oven. Grandma placed the square brass hearth-stand in front of the roaring fire, with the Dutch oven on top of it. This was like a large biscuit tin without a lid, the inside placed open to the fire. On the base a thick slice of bread was placed, with a big slice of cheese on top. Several hooks, fixed to the top of the Dutch oven, held the ends of rashers of bacon or ham which, as they hung down dropped fat on the cheese. This melted, soaking into the bread which got toasted round the edges and was deliciously crisp.

****

One Sunday morning I was awakened about six o'clock by voices with unfamiliar accents coming from downstairs. I crept down the open staircase to the snug entrance, which was halfway along the passage, where, wide-eyed, I hid on seeing my mother coming from the door leading to the kitchen. She was carrying a tray with teapot, two cups and saucers, sugar, milk and a plate piled high with bread and cheese.

Curious, but not yet daring to show myself, I became unpleasantly aware of the smell of cigarette smoke, fumes of the uncleaned stove, aroma of beer and spirits from the previous night's drinking, hanging in the air. The ash from pipes and cigarettes spattered the squarish flagstones which bore the dried, round, black stains of beer and port wine, spilled from trays carried from the bar to the smoke room, throughout Saturday. These voices drew me. I *must* see these mysterious visitors!

"There, my dear. Come and have some breakfast." Grandma was speaking to a shabby, frightened young couple who sat close together on the settle, holding hands. Grandma's smile was full of compassion for the young man and his sweetheart who had eloped from Ireland the night before. The Fishguard-London Express sometimes stopped at Landore, so they had left the train, hoping to escape from any angry relatives who might have caught the train and hoped to find them when it reached London. Grandma saw me.

"Go back to bed at once! You'll catch your death on those cold flagstones."

I had stepped out into the passage and was peeping in at the door, my bare toes curling up as the coarse coconut matting prickled my bare feet. Grandma bustled me back to bed. How romantic! I thought, ignoring the pitiful shabbiness of the reality. I *did* hope they would live happily ever after.

****

When Grandma was dressed for chapel or to go shopping in Swansea there was only one word to describe her: elegant. From the age of eight it was my privilege to accompany her on Saturday mornings, by tram, to Swansea. Dressed entirely in black from the ribbon or feather-trimmed bonnet to her toes, she wore only the best quality clothes. Her cape of heavy material with leaf-shaped pieces of doeskin, appliqued, each piece edged with jet that shone like coal in firelight, had a pleated frill of ninon or crepe-de-chine that ran round the whole cape, under which flowed a full skirt that half hid her elastic-sided boots.

Our first visit was to the market for a farm-produced chicken. Grandma looked over the displays until we came to a stall she fancied, where she pricked chicken after chicken with a pin brought especially to test for tenderness. Next: butter. There were so many tubs, the butter varying from pale to deep yellow. Grandma took a shilling from her purse to taste each sort by spooning a little with the shilling. I wondered it didn't make her sick, and how unhygienic it was of her to do so. There was a street near the market called Butter Street where other butter-sellers from the countryside farms offered their wares.

"Bore da, Mrs. Daniel." (Good-morning, Mrs. Daniel). This was the smart shop-walker's greeting as we entered the large drapery store, Edwards's. He was very imposing as he stood shaking hands with her, in his black frock coat. Pleasantly patting me on the head, he walked along with us as our progress through the shop began. Far ahead lay the wide staircase which branched off at the top into two flights, one leading to the restaurant, which we visited later for lunch; the other to the left and the millinery and lingerie departments, where the assistants seemed to me to be very old. Miss Woods, who always attended to us, wore a black gown edged round the neck by a band of white lace. It was very tight and stiffened with bones or wire so that I felt she must be choking.

"Let me show what I have for my little girl today," she said, producing pretty underwear or dresses. While she took Grandma into the millinery department to try on a new bonnet, I climbed on to a chair and wondered what to have for lunch. It was always hot pies, but there was a choice of pastries afterwards.

Lunch over, we made for the cinema, small and narrow. At the pay-desk Grandma embarrassed me by choosing the cheapest seats which were right down the front of the cinema. She made me stoop under her cape so that I looked smaller than I was and could go in for half price.

"This way, madam," and the usherette marched ahead down the aisle, flashing her torch, all of which Grandma ignored. Dragging me into one of the back rows she said "Taw son, Hannah fach (be quiet Hannah dear). She'll never find us in the dark." And somehow she never did. Whilst she enjoyed the pictures, Grandma considered she was paying what they were worth. There were several films in each performance and Grandma got confused by so many characters. She asked me what had happened to the hero in the first film in the most exciting part of the second one.

Home then with our basket full of food and me carrying my new clothes and perhaps Grandma's new bonnet. She was happy to be home so as to get those new boots off.

"Here, John, these new boots are hurting me. Wear them a bit about the house to stretch them, will you?" and my father, who had small feet, obliged. That is until one unfortunate day when he had to dash to the brewery in Swansea on business. It was in the tram, which had two long benches facing each other, that he saw two women oposite him nudging each other and giggling. Looking down he realised he was still wearing Grandma's boots. She dared not ask him to do the same favour again for a long time.

Several years later, when Evelyn and I were returning from a concert in Swansea one Saturday evening, we were surprised to meet the elegant shop-walker who had been so polite to Grandma and me, in Oxford Street, dressed in a lounge suit and trilby hat talking very loudly to a newspaper boy, who was selling the evening edition of The Cambria Daily Leader. On seeing us he stopped and, breathing whisky heavily into our astonished faces, whispered confidentially as he paid for a dozen copies of the same edition, tucking them under his arm, "Sunday tomorrow. Going to have a damn good read." We were anxious to tell Grandma how the mighty had fallen and did so, but she refused to believe a word of it.

One Saturday morning when Grandma and I had reached the tram terminus and were making our way to the market, we stopped to read a huge hoarding advertising 'Poole's Myriorama' at the Albert Hall. This was an entertainment using lantern slides, of which she approved. Anything held at the Albert Hall was acceptable to her, so we spent a few minutes in front of the hoarding while a kind gentleman pointed out some interesting bits of reading matter, as he had evidently seen the show elsewhere. It was on reaching the market that Grandma found that her purse had been stolen, no doubt by the kind gentleman as he leaned over her shoulder when explaining it all. Fortunately I had enough pennies in my little purse to take us home by tram.

Only rarely did Grandma buy clothes in the other large Swansea store, Ben Evans's, but when she failed to see a bonnet she fancied in Edwards's, we trailed along to Ben Evans's. The millinery department was on the top floor and while Grandma was trying on bonnets I climbed on a shelf to look out of the window. To my delight, what did I see, hidden behind ugly office buildings, but the turrets of a castle, Swansea Castle. I was excited about my discovery and asked my father about it when I got home. He told me that Cromwell's soldiers had been housed there during the civil strife in the seventeenth century. King Charles's men, too had stayed there. "What stories it could have told" I thought, and what a shame to hide its beauty behind such ordinary buildings.

This was remedied during the Second World War when Swansea was blitzed and the castle revealed. Standing alone among the debris it seemed as if the castle wished to point out its staying power as against modern structures.

When the time came that I felt too old for such shopping jaunts with Grandma, Dick took over from me until football became too important on Saturday mornings. Anyway, Grandma went less and less often, feeling her age. That we schoolchildren were allowed to lie in bed as long as we liked on Saturday mornings disgusted her and she would demand that Dick or I go to Jones Top Shop for floor polish or something, and we daren't disobey.

CHAPTER 10

My sister Evelyn became a music teacher and although Grandma wasn't musical she liked to listen to her playing the piano, but only to hymns and to songs like 'Into Thy hands O Lord I come'. Another favourite was 'Ora Pro Nobis' though neither Grandma nor I knew what the words meant. I suppose it was a point of strategy that I should have piano lessons from a teacher other than my sister. I began learning from a lady who to my disgust couldn't span an octave as her fingers were so short, and Evelyn could do this quite easily. I found it a long, tiresome walk to her house and when Eira also was allowed to learn the piano we both went to the popular Miss Amelia Parton.

She was a beautiful young lady who wore exquisite blouses and pretty rings and bracelets. We admired her enormously and I decided that one day I would be a music teacher and dress exactly like Miss Parton, including the lovely jewellery. Eira and I learned to play duets, our favourite being 'Sleigh Bells'. We had to wear tight elastic bracelets with tiny bells sewn on them around our wrists. These tinkled as we played and we showed off badly in front of our family and friends. Another duet was called "The Victoria Cross", a very stirring, patriotic piece.

I had another friend, Gwyneth, who attended our chapel and was very clever at playing by ear. Having taught her the vamping parts of our duets, we two also enjoyed playing them.

When asked to take part in a Band of Hope concert in the chapel we chose 'Sleigh Bells' for our joint item and I chose 'Hyacinths', my latest piece as my solo. It had three sharps, which I thought very clever to perform. But what should Gwyneth play for her solo? After considering a few of the pieces she had heard played by the cinema pianist, she decided on one with 'crossed hands', a rare achievement which she had mastered. We had no idea what the piece was called but I found a piece in the music stool in the parlour, which had a pretty cover, a charming ship on a ridiculously blue sea. It was called 'Fairy Barque' and this would do.

"What about turning over?" I asked Gwyneth doubtfully.

"When I come to the crossed hands bit I'll give you a kick and it's then you'll have to turn the page," she advised.

All went off well and, making homework as our excuse for leaving early, we escaped. Our fame must have spread as we were asked to play at a Women's Guild meeting at a nearby chapel. We were over-confident this time and the music sheet fell on to our hands soon after we had started playing. This set us off giggling and we weren't asked again.

When tired of practising scales I would sit at the piano dreaming of being a cinema pianist playing 'Hearts and Flowers' or dreamy chords for scenes of romance. For cowboy scenes, exciting galloping music thundered through the parlour.

On Saturday afternoons the local cinema allowed children in for half price. We were led to the cheapest seats right in the front; not individual seats, but long benches. These were comfortable enough at first but if it was a wet day, as it often was in the winter, and the cinema crowded with children, a man in charge came to the front with one of those long, hooked poles for closing and opening windows. This he used to push us closer and closer together, so that we could hardly breathe. The films were silent except for the piano accompaniment, and one particularly wet day there flashed on the screen an announcement:

"Send your children to the Landore Cinema on Saturday afternoons where they will be comfortable and well-looked after."

All the children were reading this aloud and at the end Gwyneth shouted "Yes, and have a poke with Old Olly's stick!" If we hadn't been sitting in the middle of the front row we would have been sent out.

****

Grandma's ideas about right and wrong were very rigid and she was convinced that she was always right regarding ethics. Playing-cards were 'an instrument of the devil', and not allowed at The Station Inn. But unknown to her there were cards there and games played. To accomplish this was a risky business. The kitchen door led into the middle kitchen or smoke-room where those who wanted a game of dominoes could sit in comfort at the large table. Although not actively concerned in running the inn, Grandma liked to show her authority by making a tour of the 'business' once every evening.

For a while she would be darning or reading, as it was a sin to be idle, and I did my homework. The moment I saw her put her sewing or book away I knew the time for inspection had come. I darted into the smoke-room to give my father the warning he had been watching for throughout the card game being played. Like lightning, the long drawer in the table was opened, the cards, cribbage board and used matchsticks swept inside and the drawer quickly but quietly shut.

Meanwhile a game of dominoes would be set up and, to all appearances concentrating on the game the customers would look up and give a polite "Good-eve-ning, Mrs. Daniel" as Grandma passed through the smoke-room to the bar. She ignored the customers in the snug as she considered it unseemly for women to be drinking in a public house. Through the open door came the hot smell of mulled beer, prepared in the red hot fire. A cone-shaped metal tun-dish which I saw being washed and cleaned until gleaming every Saturday morning, was plunged at the pointed end into the middle of the fire, with three-quarters of a pint of beer placed in it. The rest of the beer lay in the glass tankard with a knob of butter, a pinch of nutmeg and some fine sandy brown sugar, all thoroughly mixed. When the tun-dish was taken out of the fire, the narrow pointed end was always red-hot, which showed it was ready, and the beer was poured into the pint and again mixed. You had to pay a halfpenny more for a pint of mulled beer. It was considered very good for curing colds. I tasted some once and thought it horrid. Years later when I was ill I was given some hot elderberry wine which had exactly the same taste.

One customer liked to heat his half-pint of beer by plunging a red hot poker into it. It made a hissing noise which alarmed me. Those who paid for mulled beer thought this customer was too mean to pay the extra halfpenny.

Although sharp in her tongue Grandma was always kind. My parents were indulgent. When my father heard of children being severely punished he would say:

"You should give little ones all the love you can. The old world will punish them enough one day."

When I heard a friend's mother speak sharply to her one day I felt, "If Mama ever spoke to me like that I'd break my heart."

****

When I heard my mother say "Kissing a man without a moustache is like eating an egg without salt," I couldn't understand it, since when my father kissed me goodnight the way his moustache tickled my cheek was not at all pleasant and certainly not romantic. As for eggs without salt, that was just the way I liked my breakfast egg!

Grandma was convinced that no man could be considered handsome unless he had a beard and side-burns, or 'sideboards' as she called them. These were strongly evident in every one of the photographs of men in the thick, heavy, black family album on the parlour table.

Their suits were made of coarse material, with high collars, white and stiffly-starched, so that they must have been very uncomfortable to wear. The women all wore summer dresses and carried a closed parasol. The general expression in every photograph was serious or frightened: never smiling. This was possibly due to the unnerving sight of the cumbersome camera and paraphernalia, especially the black material the photographer placed over his head when taking the photograph.

****

There was a bicycle with no saddle in the inn yard. Having mastered a short ride across the yard I wanted to practise jumping off. I jumped off quite well but landed on the metal saddle which gave me a terrible pain at the base of my spine. I dared not tell anyone as I had been forbidden to ride the 'bone-shaker', though I was to suffer for this for years when doing P.T. at school.

Outside the back door stood a huge water butt for catching rainwater, supposed to be good for the complexion. Next to it was a small coal shed which was thickly covered in snow in winter. As Shrove Tuesday drew near, Dick and I prayed that it would snow the night before as we always had snow-pancakes on Pancake Day for tea. I can see (even now) Grandma, scooping a basin full of snow from the roof of the shed and it was this she used, with a little milk, for the pancakes. When I told a girl in my class this, she laughed and didn't believe me. I was relieved, years later, when I heard a radio cook saying you could use snow for making pancakes.

Adjacent to our kitchen door, leading to the back door, was a small room no bigger than a box room. After opening the kitchen door you saw on your left the door to the back yard. Facing you and against the wall stood a food safe with a door of wire netting. Here were kept the butter, meat, milk and eggs. To the right, a doorway led to the brewhouse, a narrow room with a flagged stone floor on which stood a large deal table where Dick and I made toffee on wet Saturday afternoons, if we could find enough brown sugar, with varying degrees of success. A long, deep wall-trough ran from the doorway almost to the tiny window which looked on to the yard; we called this the cooler. Into it was flung the dirty clothes ready for the washerwoman who came on Mondays, when the brewhouse became full of steam from the boiler in which the clothes were washed. It stood next to a deal bench with the zinc bath and scrubbing board on top of it. That trough must have been used for the process of brewing long ago. I cried, "Grandma, come and see Mrs. Jones's hands. They look dead. All white and crinkled up." I was reassured when our washerwoman came into the kitchen for her bread and cheese and bottle of stout to see that her hands were growing pinker and that she seemed all right. "Too much washing clothes in too hot water, too often," was Grandma's explanation. I couldn't take my eyes off those hands.

****

There was a woman who often came into Eira's mother's grocery shop to buy oatmeal from the large bowl on the counter. She would start eating it there in the shop and Eira's mother said she had a craving for it, saying it was good for the complexion. She was a very pale-faced woman with black hair, which we thought attractive. When Grandma caught me eating a spoonful of oatmeal from the packet on the kitchen table, she was very cross.

"What's the use of dosing you with iron for your blood when here you are, drying it all up with oatmeal, if you please."

I told her about the woman and her remark was:

"No wonder she looks so pasty. Anyway, this oatmeal is for cooking the laverbread" and suiting the action to the word she tossed some oatmeal thickly on the mound of black laverbread to be fried in the bacon fat for our breakfast. Grandma explained that laverbread is made from a particular species of seaweed and that it is full of iodine, something also good for me as I was so anaemic. I didn't like the idea that it came from seaweed, but Uncle Alf who had travelled the world swore it was much nicer than caviare.

A favourite recipe of mine was 'teisen clorion' or potato cake. Grandma boiled double the amount of potatoes needed for dinner and left the rest to get cold. During the afternoon she added butter, sugar and eggs and perhaps milk to the potato, mixing it to a dough and rolling it out to a big, thin, flat plate-shaped piece. This was baked on the 'man' (bakestone) on top of the fire in the kitchen. It appeared on the tea table spread with plenty of butter and cut into slices. I thought it the most delicious tea in the world and when my mother was preparing my birthday party I insisted on having potato-cake in addition to the jelly, blancmange and pastries. It must have been an uncommon dish as my young friends refused to even try it.

"What's it made of?"

"Potato."

"Ugh. Potato? No, I don't think I'd like potato for tea." It may be only so delicious in retrospect, but since growing up I have never yet succeeded in making potato-cake like Grandma used to make.

****

Every summer Grandma took me to spend a holiday among her Pryce relatives. We went by train to Pantyffynon, where a horse and trap met us to take us the few miles to Capel Hendre. This was the village where her brother William's sons and their wives, his daughters and their husbands, and their many children lived. It was no wonder that someone once called it Prycetown.

I clung to Grandma as we jolted along to the top of a hill and then down into the village. First one child would catch sight of us, then a shout brought more children out to the road.

By the time we had stopped outside Auntie Rahcel's house the trap was surrounded by children shouting the news, "Mae Doris wedi dod" (Doris has come). Greetings and hugs would bring us to 'Bronhaul' where I would be left for my two weeks' holiday. The eldest daughter, Annie, was my age and my great friend. These folk were very dear to Grandma. Wasn't her brother William's eldest son the rightful heir to the Estate?

In a compact little terrace of houses lived Grandma's nieces and nephews and their children. The men worked in the collieries whose mineral rights, they were convinced, should be theirs and not in the hands of Chancery. Grandma's conversation with the nephews inevitably involved the Estate and plans for recovering the property. When the trap came to take Grandma back to the station I couldn't help feeling abandoned in spite of the warm welcome and the thrill of being with Annie again. I couldn't sleep the first night because of the silence. I was used to trains rushing past The Station Inn and the shunting of trucks in the night. So I lay awake night after night, breathing in the unfamiliar scent of new-mown hay.

All sorts of treats were arranged for the little town girl, including haymaking on nearby farms. One farm from which I fetched fresh milk in a big jug every evening was called, surprisingly for such a Welsh area, 'Morning Star' and another, 'Waterloo'. I was invited to have dinner at Uncle Lewis's one day and the next at Aunty Deborah's, where there were always large plates of blackberry and apple tarts lying on the flagstone shelf, cooling, so that we could have them after the chicken dinner. Supper would be at Auntie Mary's, with more delicious food.

It was certainly a shock to burst into Uncle Isaac's kitchen and see him, stark naked, having a bath in the huge zinc tub in front of the fire. I never knew one uncle from another when they walked up the road from work as they all looked the same, covered in coal-dust. I was careful before rushing into the kitchen when bath time came after that, though no one else was shocked. This was the daily ritual.

On Sundays we all went to chapel where my cousin Frank, Uncle Isaac's eldest son, played the violin to accompany the hymns. But I was homesick. I missed my friend Eira and going into Swansea. To spend an evening in the cinema at Ammanford meant walking miles there and back. No trams: just Shank's pony. It nearly 'killed' me. Once was enough and not worth the effort.

While Annie was helping Auntie Rachel with the housework and her many children, I spent a lot of time in the parlour. Since I could play the piano fairly well by this time, the parlour had become my sanctum. A picture above the piano depressed me, though. It showed a poor woman in a very thin robe clinging to a wobbly cross in a stormy sea, her eyes frantically beseeching heaven to save her from the tossing waves.

I wrote letters home, many letters.

"Dear Mama,

It was raining yesterday. We had peas, kidney beans and ffa (broad beans) for breakfast, all boiled together and mixed with butter. I helped the boys to pick them last night. For dinner we had chicken and apple tart and cream. For supper I went to Auntie Polly's. We had cold meat and apple tart."

Letter after letter ran like that: simple menus of our meals. I was breaking my heart but how could I let on? Auntie Rachel used to read my letters before I posted them, and they were all so kind to me. Painfully homesick I had an idea. I wrote the usual letter, leaving room at the end for a few lines, showed it to Auntie and took it, unsealed to the post office, but didn't go inside. Resting my letter on the window sill outside I scribbled:

"Please Dada come and fetch me home. It's so quiet here and the lav. is such a long way up the garden." Happily I posted my letter and waited.

Two days later came the same trap with Grandma and my father. I heard their voices and hid in the parlour trying to conceal my happiness as Uncle Isaac and Auntie Rachel went out to meet them. With joy I heard Grandma's voice.

"It was such a lovely morning that John and I thought we'd come and see you all. And how is my big girl behaving herself?" I crept out of the parlour, all my love and thankfulness pouring out as Grandma hugged me.

"Perhaps now that we are here we could take Hannah fach back with us," she suggested deceitfully, as though the idea had just struck her. "It would save another journey, wouldn't it?" I tried hard to look sorry, but interjected eagerly:

"If Annie can come with us." So it was hurriedly arranged, a basket-work case packed for her and off we set for home, sweet home. It was a thrill for Annie, just watching the trains roaring past, and bliss for me to be back in smoky Landore. Annie was quite happy, sitting on the doorstep for hours, until Grandma had to tell her she was in the way of customers wanting to come in. So we'd sit at the window of the front bedroom which was on a level with the railway. Sometimes people waved to us from stationary trains.

Annie had a sweet soprano voice and loved to listen to Evelyn playing the piano, la-la-ling the tune if she didn't know the words. Even if it was a 'voluntary' for the chapel service where Evelyn had become organist, Annie would trill away.

I longed to take Annie to Mumbles on the famous train, with the 'Puffing Billy' engine, said to be the oldest in Britain. I promised that we would sit on the top deck that was open to all the cinders that flew from the engine, but the thrill of riding along so near the edge of the sea shouldn't be missed. Day after day it rained so we couldn't go until Sunday, when it was beautifully fine and the very day for a trip to the seaside.

Grudgingly we were allowed to go. It was a strange experience for me to be walking through the town on a Sunday without going to chapel service. As we waited to cross the road at the 'Slip', as the entrance to Swansea sands was called, we could see the train coming, crowded with people, all taking advantage of the sudden bright weather. The train stopped at the 'Slip' and we quickly crossed the road to climb aboard. But here, in that few minutes walk, in the sight and hearing of all those people, we were pointed to and shouted at by none other than 'Holy Joe', the well-known and respected preacher at street corners.

"Look at them" he shouted, "sinners both of them, gallivanting to the Mumbles on the Sabbath when they should be attending a place of worship. Shame on you!"

We were glad to get lost among the other sinners and forgot our shame in the joy of the glorious bays and beaches around those lumpy rocks, the Mumbles.

HAIKU - THE MUMBLES

Twin rounded rocks
a woman's breasts resemble,
thus "mamelles" becomes - Mumbles.

Unused to being free to do as she liked, Annie was always anxious to wash up and help the servant. This gave me a guilty feeling, as it never occurred to me to do so. At home, Annie had to work hard, taking the burden of housework from her mother, who always seemed to be sitting in her kitchen nursing the newest baby. Aunty Rachel was a very pretty woman with bright blue eyes and a serene manner, and she bore eleven children.

Curly hair being the fashion, it was ironical and I thought very unfair that all of Annie's brothers had fair curls and deep dimples, while she and her sister had straight hair.

Some years later, I went for a short holiday to Capel Hendre, staying as usual at 'Bronhaul'. The very first night I was awakened by much stirring in the house, voices and hurrying up and down the stairs. In the morning I learned that Auntie had had yet another baby. A little girl with blue eyes, fair curly hair and dimples. The wrong had been righted. We were sitting in the kitchen, silent, listening to the tiny noises of the crying baby upstairs. One of the boys, Glyn, about sixteen years old, was reading at the table when Uncle came down with a bundle in his arms. Before I could get up to look at the baby, Glyn slammed his book shut and, as he left the room said:

"Disgusting I call it."

The overmantel in the parlour at 'Bronhaul' was draped with Annie's Eisteddfod prizes for singing. The mirror was almost entirely obscured by the many dangling ribbons, with pretty little purses made of red or purple satin or velvet attached to them. A red purse would have a purple satin baby-ribbon strap; a purple purse would have a bright yellow one. They had contained the prize money, usually sixpenny pieces I was told, but this had been spent long since.

I recalled these when, many years later, I was teaching in London. Each St. David's Day I nostalgically held an Eisteddfod in my class of seven-year-olds, to the amusement of the rest of the staff, who asked one year if their children might join my Eisteddfod. It became so popular that it ended in my having half the school trying for the unusual prizes. Of course I made little purses of any pieces of silk or velvet I could find, with patent fasteners, to enclose the sixpences with long, baby ribbon straps. All the winners were delighted when I hung the ribbon round their necks, like mayoral chains, with the unknown prizes hidden inside.

What the Cockney mums made of their offsprings' prizes I never knew. Perhaps they thought it just a whim of that Welsh teacher. But for me, the morning of 'March the First' took me straight back to Auntie Rachel's parlour in Capel Hendre and all the talk of the Estate, or as my Grandma called it 'Y Stat'. And the music I played for my little ones to walk into assembly was "The March of the Men of Harlech", greeted by smiles from the rest of the staff.

CHAPTER 11

Whilst I spent my summer holidays in Capel Hendre, my cousins Ray and Gwen and my sister Evelyn had a much more glamorous fortnight with Grandma at Llandrindod Wells, the spa where she 'took the waters'. She was up early every morning and off to the Pump Room to buy her half pint of sulphur or saline water. The girls told me it tasted horrible, but Grandma was convinced it did her the world of good. I looked forward to their return to hear all about the beautiful spa, the pierrots and other entertainments. Gradually I grew disenchanted with Capel Hendre and nagged Grandma to take me to Llandrindod.

"You shall come, Hannah fach, perhaps next summer."

Grandma always brought presents for all of us, and not only for us but for neighbours' children too. Once she produced from her big trunk something wrapped in tissue paper that I knew must be a doll for me. She held it up: a beautiful doll with blue eyes, fair curls and a long, pink satin dress down to its toes.

I held out my arms for it, but she said,

"Wait a minute. Watch this." And, holding the doll upside down, the dress fell back and a golliwog appeared dressed in a red and white striped jacket. I could hardly wait to hug it, but again Grandma held me away from her saying, "This is for Florrie." My face fell; but surely she had brought one for me too! From the trunk she lifted a parcel which was certainly not a doll; more likely a book or a box of chocolates. I couldn't hide my disappointment when I read the title, "Stories of Jesus". I ran upstairs, threw the book on the floor, and flung myself on the bed in tears.

****

Miss Parton now thought I could play the piano well enough to compete in an Eisteddfod in Swansea. I practised the set pieces until the dreaded day when my father took me along to perform before the adjudicator. With us went another of Miss Parton's pupils, who was also accompanied by her father, a Mr. Davies. Hovering about in the entrance hall were several other ten-year olds, equally nervous no doubt.

"Oh dear" exclaimed Mr. Davies, "look who's adjudicating! See the girl by the door, the one in the green dress? Well, she's the adjudicator's niece. Our girls haven't got a hope of winning." And of course, neither of us won.

That was the only Eisteddfod at which I ever competed, but the other girl, Dilys, went on to make music-teaching her very successful career. I gave up having lessons after this but never stopped playing the piano in our parlour, and eventually Evelyn and I were able to play duets as she was given an organ for her birthday. It was the same pitch as the piano and sounded, we thought like a small orchestra, with Dick pumping away with varying spurts of energy.

Our parlour was a crowded room now that we had the organ, the piano, two easy chairs and the big round table with its dark green fringed cloth, hymn-book and heavy photograph albums. I had seen a 'What-Not' in a friend's parlour, its shelves covered with tiny 'coats of arms' of Tenby, Aberystwyth and such resorts. I bought one of Swansea for Grandma and decided that one day I would have a 'What-Not' filled with them. But my gift was put in a cupboard out of the way.

****

Our street was full of Joneses. There was Jones Top Shop and Jones Bottom Shop, Mrs. Jones the Post (her late husband had been a postman, Mrs. Jones Harry (who had a son called Harry) and Mrs. Jones Mabel (after her daughter). There were endless Joneses but right in the middle of the row came a surprisingly English name: Mrs. Preston.

On New Year's Day the local children went from house to house and shop to shop to wish the occupants a Happy New Year. I used to take Dick along and almost before we entered a shop he was given his reward of an orange, an apple or a penny, so utterly engaging was his happy little face, fair hair and blue eyes. The previous day my father would have gone to the bank for five shilling's worth of new pennies for the children, mainly customers' children who came to greet Grandma. These coins were special and shone like gold. Dick and I were reluctant to spend these new pennies; they were so pretty and looked worth much more.

Among the Joneses was one nicknamed 'Freddie Fruppence', the only child of a widow. He was the leader in every bit of mischief and Dick liked to play with him. One wet Saturday afternoon we joined Freddie and some other children, forming a group at the junction of two roads, in pouring rain. We stood under Freddie's umbrella and sang hymns from his father's best hymnbook. We giggled as we sang, the rain dripping from the umbrella all over us as we made a horrible din. We thought it great fun until his mother appeared in her doorway.

"Here you are, is it? And with your poor father's best umbrella!" she stormed as she dragged Freddie into the house, clouting him with the umbrella and leaving us soaking wet. "And his hymnbook too!"

"We were only playing Salvation Army," Freddie blubbered.

"I'll give you Salvation Army indeed,' she shouted as she slammed the door.

Dick and I were only too glad to sneak unnoticed into the

brewhouse, where we rubbed our hair with the first towel among the washing.

Freddie got his nickname from an earlier incident during the summer holidays. While other children were able to get to the sands and bays, he hadn't the tram fare, and there he was sitting on his doorstep with no one to play with. It was that quiet time in the street when babies have their afternoon nap, giving their mothers a rest. The silence was shattered by the cry of the rag and bone man, leading his horse and cart piled with old clothing up the road.

Not a soul was about as the man plodded along, making for the inn on the corner where he was in the habit of spending at least ten minutes each time he made his round. Freddie knew this and as soon as he felt the man would be well into his half pint, he got up and strolled casually towards the cart. Cautiously glancing around to see there was no one looking, he grabbed an armful of rags from the top of the pile and ran up the road. In the doorway of a lock-up shop he waited, the rags hidden behind his back. After what seemed an hour the sound of trotting hoofs told him the cart was coming past his way. Freddie let it go by perhaps fifteen yards, then ran after it shouting that he had some rags from his mother. Fuddled, the rag and bone man did not recognise the nondescript rags, flung them on to the cart and gave Freddie threepence. After this story got around Freddie was for evermore called Freddie Fruppence.

Grandma was very cross when she heard that Dick was involved with Freddie and two other boys in harassing people. They would sit on the pavement, two each side, facing each other. Freddie and his bosom pal held a rope, stretched across the road, about six inches from the ground. As soon as they saw anyone approaching they called out 'Mind the rope!' and of course people stepped carefully over it. Meanwhile further down the road, Dick sat on one side of the pavement facing another boy, but with no rope, and shouted 'Mind the rope!' at passers by. Everybody lifted a foot and the boys screamed with laughter at this.

****

After an illness of many months it was misery returning to school again. Most of my friends had been working hard in preparation for the Scholarship examination in a few months time. I didn't know whether I wanted to try the examination or not. It was hard enough trying to catch up with the rest of the class in the ordinary work. The girls who weren't considered bright enough went to housewifery classes which included cookery, laundry work and, once a week, a swimming lesson in the Swansea Baths. So to my disgrace I was put among this group. I hated the cookery lessons, although I came home one day triumphantly with flaky pastry apple-tartlets I had made, and over which the family raved. They were nicer than Grandma's lardy tarts. Laundry, too, was a real burden to me. One day the contraption for drying clothes, which hung high above us, collapsed and dropped on top of me. I was like an animal in a wooden trap. I was sent home with an older girl to explain to my parents what had happened. I was only very slightly bruised and shaken and was delighted, as it meant no more laundry lessons for me.

As for the swimming lessons, the hard, masculine-faced woman who taught us terrified me. We shivered, holding on to the rail, waiting in turn for the individual lesson. I slyly moved behind her, turning my face away so she wouldn't notice I hadn't had my turn, and now I was among those already tested. I escaped learning to swim, which I have regretted all my life since. Among this group there was one girl who was always in trouble with our teacher for being naughty. One swimming day she disgusted the instructor by flinging off her wet swimsuit and, instead of drying herself and getting dressed, ran out on to the edge of the pool and danced round naked and singing a very common song, popular at the time. Whether or not she was punished I never knew, as I was suddenly relieved of those ghastly cookery and swimming lessons, as well as the laundry work.

I must have picked up pretty well in my class work by this time as my teacher gave me a letter to give to my parents, saying my work had improved so much that she thought I had a chance of passing the Scholarship examination if I worked hard. Would I? I'd work like anything to be with my friends again and escape the chores. The really clever ones passed to the High School. I just managed to get into the Municipal Secondary School.

When the result came through I flew home on wings to tell my family I'd passed, only to find that they already knew. To my angry disappointment the girl next door had run before me and told them. I could have killed her as I knew what a thrill it would have given them, knowing how doubtful my chances of passing were. She was the girl who had been given the wonderful doll by Grandma and I had never forgiven her for that.

When Dick was old enough to sit the Scholarship exam, he wanted to know if he might have a bike if he passed. Somehow I never saw Dick up to his eyes in homework, yet he got through his examinations all right. The day he was told he had passed he rushed home and the first thing he said was,

"Now can I have my bike? I've passed the Scholarship."

****

The story Miss Jones was reading to us was 'Bluebeard', and at the end she asked "Has anyone ever seen a man with a blue beard?" We all said 'No' and smiled at the idea.

"Or a beard of any other colour than brown or black?" In all innocence I said I'd seen a man with a green beard, which sent the whole class laughing and me blushing madly.

"Where did you see this man with the green beard?" Miss Jones asked kindly.

"On my way home from school."

I was quite right. The man worked in the copper-works where the chemical used had stained his fair beard, green.

****

A few doors from Eira's grocer-shop lived a little girl named Dolly. She was just like a pretty fairy doll and when she became seriously ill we were all sad. She died of pneumonia. It was the usual thing to visit houses where a child had died, so Eira and I went to see Dolly, lying in her small coffin like an angel. We gazed at the waxen figure and before coming away we touched her cold little hand so that we wouldn't dream about her. This touching was a kind of magic, but it was what was done by everyone at that time.

****

Tuesday meant sewing lesson and having to buy a thimble at the draper's on the way to school.

"You want another halfpenny, I suppose?" Grandma grumbled. I lost my thimble regularly on the way home, but I had to have one. These were dreary lessons as we were given very small pieces of coarse calico to work with. There was endless hemming to be done in minute stitches and unpicked again and again if too large. The material was filthy by the time I had finished and there was no end-product, though an attempt was made at our making dresses. The material was 'brown Holland' and the pattern very ordinary. Eira and I were used to having pretty little dresses made by our mothers, who had both been trained as dressmakers when young girls. I never wore the resultant sack I had made; neither did Eira. Grandma was disgusted not only with the messy work I had done but with the poor material.

While we were sewing in class the teacher invariably read us a story. I loved this but also dreaded it as she chose such sad ones that made me cry. Strangling the tears in my throat I went home with a raging headache every Tuesday. My anguish was added to by Florrie, sitting next to me. She sobbed shamelessly, especially when it was the story about Little Dot, a child of seven who became very ill and died. If Florrie hadn't cried so pitiably I could have held my tears back. Altogether she was a blooming nuisance in my life; she hung round me wherever I went.

"We don't want her, she isn't our type,"Eira would argue. Of course when I got home Grandma had heard all about this and I was told off for being snobbish and unkind. How could I make grown-ups understand that children like to choose their own friends? Besides, Florrie sometimes came to school wearing the cast-off dresses too shabby for me to wear and I felt embarrassed for her, though she didn't seem to mind that my friends recognised them. At meal times she would suddenly appear, standing quietly at our kitchen door, watching us eating.

"Shouldn't you be at home having your tea, Florrie?" my mother asked.

"My mother sent me in here out of the way, as they are having their tea," she explained, innocently honest. In spite of the unwelcoming expressions on our faces, Grandma invariably chose a piece of cake and handed it to Florrie, who wouldn't disappear even then.

"Can I find the pins on the floor, Mrs. Matthews?" she asked, having seen my mother stitching away on the Singer sewing machine earlier. This was a way, I suppose, of justifying her being there and in return for the piece of cake. It was always a big piece, a treat for her, I expect. Grandma had a large heart, embracing all around.

Little boys wore dresses until they were sometimes four years old and when Florrie's brothers reached three my mother would sort out Dick's little suits with which to 'britch' them in turn. This was quite a ceremony which took place on a Sunday morning. The little boy was brought into our kitchen in his dress and then fitted out in one of Dick's 'grown-out-of' blouses and a pair of trousers. Dick would then take him home to his mother to show off his new clothes. He had been 'britched'. His dress was discarded for evermore and he was now a real boy.

Florrie's mother, in spite of all the work she had to do was always willing to lend a hand when there was a servant shortage at The Station Inn and she was a good neighbour. All our neighbours were kind. I remember when we had fish for dinner we had to go to ask Mrs. Hitchings if she would let us have some fennel. We would follow her up the long, narrow garden path to the patch of fennel. We never paid for this. Grandma may have had some arrangement with Mrs. Hitchings over this; a bottle of pop in exchange for the herb perhaps; I never knew but I suspect it was given with a willing heart and no payment expected or demanded. All this was much appreciated as we had no garden of any kind, just the yard.

The yard was fine for playing hide and seek behind the empty beer-barrels. Dick and his friends played 'cat and dog' with pieces of stick. One very short piece was laid on the ground and struck by the other stick with such force that it flew up in the air and away. I don't know if there were any rules in this game except perhaps that the owner of the stick who shot furthest was the winner. Girls were never seen playing 'cat and dog'. I know I never did. Having a big yard was a great advantage. We could bring all our friends there where there was no grass to 'keep off'.

My favourite game was 'In and out the windows'. For this one chosen girl stood in the middle of a large ring formed by the rest of us, boys and girls with linked hands, while we sang:

"In and out the windows, In and out the window,
In and out the windows, as you have done before."

The chosen girl danced in and out of the ring, under our arms, stopping at the end of the tune, in the middle of the ring, now we sang while she danced in the same way:

'Stand and face your lover, Stand and face your lover,
"Stand and face your lover, as you have done before."

The girl then stood in front of the boy she had chosen. Shyly he took her hand and they walked together round the ring, ready to dance while we sang:

"Take her off to Cardiff, Take her off to Cardiff,
Take her off to Cardiff, as you have done before."

Reversing, they danced round the ring on the outside, while we sang:

"Bring her back to Swansea
Bring her back to Swansea
Bring her back to Swansea,
As you have done before."

They re-entered the ring. Vigorously they shook hands as we sang the last verse:

"Shake hands before you leave her, Shake hands before you leave her.
Shake hands before you leave her, As you have done before."

The romance was over for these two. The girl joined the ring and the boy in turn chose his lover which, to us, meant sweetheart.

****

There was a small shed in the yard which was not used because a huge slab of stone almost filled it, leaning precariously against one of the walls. But we liked to play 'house' there, placing pretty pieces of china or coloured glass from broken bottles lying about on top of the stone slab, as if it were a dresser.

One day Evelyn and a friend were passing through the yard. Evelyn glanced inside the shed and, noticing the shining objects on our 'dresser', squeezed herself inside and stretched up to reach the top of the slab. Her weight brought the heavy stone towards her, threatening to crush her against the opposite wall, her friend screamed and started pushing the slab back with all her strength. Soon her cries brought help and Evelyn was removed with only a few scratches to show for it.

Everyone in Landore was told how her life had been saved by her friend; how she would have been crushed to death by a stone weighing at least a ton. As time went on, that stone increased in weight until it became a two-ton stone, according to the account given by Evelyn's heroic friend. This put an end to our playing 'house' in the shed, since a lock was put on it, which was a pity.

****

We were told to call Mary Jane, my father's sister, 'Auntie Mary' after Dick had greatly embarrassed her one day when he was sent to meet her train. As soon as he saw her face at the compartment window he shouted 'Auntie Mary Jane'. This drew smiles from the people in her compartment, which annoyed her.

I spent several holidays at her lovely home which was run like a hospital, it was so scrupulously clean. She had been a hospital matron before her marriage to Uncle J.W. as we called him. She never called him John or Jack like my mother called my father. It was always J.W.

Auntie Mary was a social worker and took me with her to visit sick people in the village. I carried the basket with calves foot jelly and chicken broth and noticed with pride how respectful these people were towards her. I watched her making pastry which was so much nicer than Grandma's which was mixed in a bowl. Auntie Mary simply put the flour on the pastry board and quickly mixed it with water and sometimes an egg. It was always as light as a feather.

She did beautiful art-needlework and once a fortnight went to Cardiff for lessons. In the week between, these sessions were held in Auntie's house, the teacher coming from Cardiff. Other ladies from the village, the doctors' wives, the bank-manager's wife and the headmasters' wives came to the house. On these occasions I was allowed to hand around sandwiches and cakes while the lesson proceeded. For some reason, most of Auntie's embroidered pictures are scenes containing peacocks, spreading their colourful tails.

Dick and I spent a holiday at Auntie Mary's house once. We were rather awed by the grandeur of this private house compared to The Station Inn where, apart from the private rooms, there were flagstones everywhere, not to mention sawdust on the floor of the bar. We dreaded breakfast time as Uncle J.W. asked Dick to say Grace. Dick blushed and mumbled 'Be present at our table, Lord'. Next day I had to say Grace and I repeated Dick's words. After that, Uncle took over, varying his phrases, and I wished I could have thought of different words.

We all went to chapel whatever the weather, taking a torch for the evening service to help us negotiate the rough road. Uncle sat in the 'Big seat'. He was a deacon, as were two of his brothers who lived locally. The minister usually came back with us for supper and later we sang hymns in harmony, my young aunt accompanying and singing too.

I was very impressed one Sunday morning after chapel when Auntie Mary took me into the house of a lady who was the sister of Dr. Tom Jones, private secretary to Mr. David Lloyd George. Some years later when we called on her, she took me into the parlour and showed me a cupboard where, she said, very important state papers were hidden all through the First World War.

It was during this visit that I had the most bewildering and unhappy experience of my young life. I had gone on my own to stay at Auntie Mary's and Uncle J.W's home. Had Dick been with me it would have been more upsetting than it was. Brought up as we were I had not had the facts of life explained to me either by my mother or my sister who was five years my senior.

Here in this grand house I slept alone in a small bedroom next door to that of my aunt and uncle. It was an exceptionally cold night and I was glad of the earthenware hot water bottle which I hugged. About midnight, Auntie came into my room and told me that their hot-water bottle had burst and asked if I would mind if they slept in my bed. I could share Sarah's bed. Shivering, I followed Auntie Mary along the corridor to the maid's bedroom and snuggled down beside her. She was up at seven and went downstairs to clean the dining room grate and lay the table for breakfast while I lay there feeling dreadfully ill and wondering what this unusual pain could be. I thought I must have caught a cold by changing beds at midnight. When at last I got up feeling languid and drained of strength I found to my dismay and horror that my nightdress and the undersheet were stained.

Something terrible had happened to me, but I simply could not tell Auntie Mary about my dilemma. She had been a hospital matron and cleanliness was her god. All I knew then was that I must clean everything up before she saw it. Somehow I managed to wash my nightdress in cold water in the wash basin and I dragged the sheet off the bed to wash the patch of stain. What now?

Had Auntie had any little girls of her own I wouldn't have hesitated to run to her with my trouble. Folding my nightdress, damp as it was, I placed it under my pillow and replaced the sheet and made up the bed to look as if nothing had happened. Then I slowly went down to breakfast. All seemed normal and cheerful except myself. I couldn't eat anything and daren't move from my chair. Within half an hour I saw Sarah whisper to Auntie and they both left for the kitchen. Auntie Mary took me upstairs to the bathroom where she said severely:

"I can give you some towels, but you shouldn't have come away unprepared when you were expecting your period."

So that's what it was! I longed to be with my mother and the last few days dragged on endlessly. As soon as I entered the kitchen of the dear old Station Inn I rushed into my mother's arms and cried and cried. For some reason I begged my mother not to tell Evelyn about it. That I had to discover this terrific physical change when alone and away from home was to me unforgivable. I'm sure my mother felt she couldn't forgive herself either and she was particularly sweet to me.

CHAPTER TWELVE

Grandma's ambition was for Evelyn to marry a minister, but Evelyn and this young man from our chapel had their own ideas, and he married a very nice young lady, with whom my sister became great friends.

Resigned to the collapse of her plans, Grandma saw in one of the clerks in our solicitor's office a suitable partner for Evelyn. He was a likeable young man who always appeared to have been recently tubbed and scrubbed, and who smelled of Cuticura soap, but Evelyn wasn't crazy about him. In fact, on evenings when they had arranged to meet in Swansea, she insisted on my going along too. So there we were, a young couple and a reluctant schoolgirl, strolling along the Promenade. I was bored stiff and I'm sure the young man was wishing me far away so that he could be alone with Evelyn. I couldn't see why she went out with him if she didn't like him enough, but perhaps she was too kind to snub him and this was the only way she could face an evening in his company.

The meetings became fewer and fewer and then she met the love of her life whom she eventually married and I was her bridesmaid.

****

That Britain was at war against the Germans under the wicked 'Kaiser Bill' was a fact we knew only from the newspapers. It was something going on in far-away Flanders: that is until the day we were suddenly made aware of it when my cousin Glyn Daniel called to wish us all goodbye, explaining as he stood in our kitchen in his army uniform that he was going to the front.

To think that Glyn Daniel our cousin, who used to escort Evelyn and Ray to dances in his dinner-jacket, looking so elegant, might be killed or wounded, was a horrifying thought. The war was brought home to us again more closely when Evelyn's fiance joined the army, as did other young men we knew.

Grandma used to be very upset on reading the war news, especially the gory details of the German atrocities in Belgium, so my parents decided to hide as much as possible from her. This was done by blaming the poor servant for using newspapers to light the fire before Grandma could read them. If there were columns my father didn't want her to see he tore them out, his excuse being that he couldn't find a spill to light his pipe.

We were advised to eat less potatoes and my mother would make little flat rissoles of boiled salted rice and fry them in the bacon fat for breakfast. I quite liked them.

We always ate butter at home and it was used for cooking, too, so I did not taste margarine until it was served on the bread at the Kardomah Cafe where we went for tea. I remarked that the 'butter' tasted nutty.

****

Evelyn was considered old enough now to give a hand in the bar on extra busy evenings. On Saturday nights she would slip out to Jones Bottom Shop for packets of chocolate almonds, one packet each for Dick and me. I knew where these packets would be hidden on a shelf in the bar and I would run downstairs in my nightie the next morning to fetch them and take them up as early as I dare. Then Dick and I would enjoy them in our beds. It couldn't have been good for us to gobble chocolates non-stop as we did, but it kept us out of the way while the immense cleaning of the 'business' proceeded on Sunday morning.

The flagged passage would be still cleanly damp as I ran into the bar. We had extra help on Sunday mornings and I remember that once I almost tripped over a young girl I hadn't seen before, scrubbing the floor. She couldn't have been more than sixteen and surprised me with, "There's nothing so pleasant as a clean floor-cloth, is there?" I looked blankly at her, my mind full of the books I had hidden to read in bed by the light of my candle.

"No, I suppose not," I answered, thinking that there were many pleasanter things than a clean floor-cloth to my mind. However, I could see something amusing about the carton of 'Monkey Brand' with its confession that 'Monkey Brand is good for cleaning but it won't wash clothes." It was used as 'Vim' is today, I expect. As I crept upstairs I began to feel guilty about that poor girl having to go out cleaning other people's houses. So young, too!

Some years later I was told that she had been killed while working in a munitions factory and I learned a little about her private life. She had lived with her grandfather who was blind and whom she tended with love and great patience. Then I recalled seeing him sitting in the sun outside their house while she went to work. I wished I had spoken to him when passing, but children don't realise that blind people can hear one passing by, even though they can't see. It would have been kind to have said a few words if only "It's a nice day" or something.

Many women were working on munitions, including my cousin Claudia whose husband was at the front with the Royal Engineers right from the beginning of the war. Claudia used to bring her little girl to the inn at six in the morning to be looked after while she was at work. The child would scream and cry when her mother left her, but was soothed by Grandma and was picked up by Claudia on her way home from work. Her job, though supervisory, was very dangerous and it grieved our hearts that she had to do it.

Women working on munitions were highly paid and rightly so, and many were able to buy fur coats; rarely seen in those days.

My mother didn't have one, but she wore a sable necklet and always a toque. All her hats were of the toque shape, the style worn by Queen Mary. These hats suited my mother well and she invariably wore a spotted veil which she pulled down over her face and knotted under her chin.

****

After chapel on summer Sunday evenings Eira and I would walk up to Llewelyn's Park where there were always plenty of young boys and girls strolling and 'making eyes at each other'. One Sunday evening I saw, strewn across the path, torn pieces of cardboard. I picked one up and saw half a girl's face. I picked up another, then another.

"Come on" called Eira, but she had to wait while I gathered every piece I could find and wrapped them in my handkerchief. When I'd get home I would piece them together, but as I walked I imagined what the result might be. Possibly the photograph of a discarded sweetheart, angrily torn up and thrown away, or perhaps that of a heartless girl whose boy-friend had walked up this very path to the quiet of the park to ease his aching heart and, in his unhappiness, destroyed her picture.

Supper over, and after carefully wiping the dirt off the pieces of photograph, I spread them on the tablecloth, much to Grandma's disgust.

"What on earth do you want with those filthy bits of paper?"

Ah, I thought; all you can see is filthy bits of paper, but I feel sure a lovely romance lies broken among these pieces. Dick helped me to put the jigsaw together. It was almost a complete photograph except for part of a hat and some hair.

"No wonder he chucked her away," remarked Dick. And I must admit that she was no oil painting.

So much for my romantic dreaming!

We all looked forward to the annual Sunday School outing or 'treat' with great excitement. It always took place on Whit-Monday, whatever the weather. On the Saturday before my young chapel friends came to The Station Inn for my father to read the barometer. If the weather promised to be fine, it meant a glorious afternoon in a field in Killay. If rain was threatened tea was held in the Sunday School Room and this was a real let down.

On the sunny Whit-Monday we all met at the chapel where we were given train tickets for the short journey from Swansea to Killay. We walked in a crocodile into Victoria Station, Swansea, and piled into the train, reserved for us. At Killay I held Dick's hand as we walked along the lane to the field where the 'treat' was held. Tea, pop, white and brown bread and butter as well as slices of fruitcake and seedcake were pressed on us by the teachers who helped on this special day. We played games, 'Kiss in the Ring' was popular with the teenagers: 'Twos and Threes' with all ages except those who were too old to run, and there were three-legged races.

We chased one another in the small wood near the field. Then we sat in rows on the grass and the minister gave us a sweet each. He had two attractive sons, admired by all the little girls, and when one of the boys wanted more sweets, shouting 'Don't be so stingy, Dad' we thought him very witty.

Tired out and ready for the slow walk along the lane, which seemed much longer now, we carried in our sticky hands bluebells, already wilted. But however tired I was, a bunch of lilac must be bought for my mother from the house we passed on the way to the station. It was on the corner of the lane and a lilac tree positively flung its branches at us. The whole day was magic for me and the very sight and smell of lilac still takes my thoughts back to Killay.

Killay was special: to me it was somewhere you could visit only on Whit Mondays at the Sunday School outing, so it came as a shock to me the day I first travelled to Llandrindod Wells with Grandma. When the train stopped at Killay I looked out of the window and couldn't believe my eyes. Yet there it was, in bold letters, KILLAY. It simply couldn't be my Killay of the lilac and bluebells. But it was, and a place you could go to any time you wished. Some of its magic died that day.

"Can I go with Eira to their Sunday School Treat to Ynystawe?" I asked Grandma. We always asked Grandma's permission to go anywhere, even though my mother and father had already said we might go.

"How can you go with them? You don't go to Eira's Sunday School."

"But I go with her to their 'Band of Hope' and the Supperintendent said I could if you are willing."

"Well, I don't know. They go up the canal in those dirty old coal barges. No, Hannah fach, I don't fancy you coming home with your best dress all smelling of coal." But I was allowed to go in the end.

Sunday School Outing to Ynystawe

The coal-barges, extra-cleaned for this especial day
in the chapel's year, disguised gaily
in draped muslin, gipsy-red, green, gold,
Cinderella-like in carnival array, awaited
laughing children with their teachers, young and old.
Gloriously terrified of a sudden lurch, then slide
into the murky canal, they gingerly stepped aboard,
the pungent, lingering reek of coal ignored.
The shallow barges slowly moved along, drawn
by nodding, plodding horses; their clip-clop
mingling with the rhythm of hymns. Steadily borne
towards fields where trestle-tables offered tea, pop
and buns that tasted different somehow there.
They played 'Kiss in the Ring' shyly; noisily
threw balls, their excited shouts shrilling into air
drenched with the grass-breath of country-side.
All over too soon: then the reluctant homeward glide
soothed by hymns, hummed now by elders, the sated
sleep of little ones, the slow sure sinking safely
into the normality of the chapel-going way.

The peaceful atmosphere of Sunday at The Station Inn flowed over into Monday morning, before the bustle of the 'business' took over. The smell of coke from the freshly-lit bar stove and the sound of sticks crackling in the grate of the smoke-room, not yet warm, crept gradually on tiptoes into the kitchen.

The table, cleared of breakfast things was spread in turn by my father's overcoat, then his best black suit for a thorough brushing before being hung upstairs in the wardrobe until the next Sunday. My mother looked up at the grandfather-clock. Yes, there was still enough time to brush her own best navy-blue costume, before the noise of heavy boots in the bar told of men returning from their early shift at the works.

Hurriedly she flicked off the few specks of fluff and carried the best clothes upstairs. These belonged to Sunday. They were sometimes referred to as 'Sunday go to meeting' clothes. To wear them to go to the cinema or the theatre was unthinkable, sacrilegious. So much so that when on the following Friday evening, my young Aunt Dorothy and her companion, or best friend, called while I was being bathed by Grandma in front of the kitchen fire, I was shocked to notice as they sat down that though they were on their way to the cinema they were wearing their chapel-going clothes.

I crouched low in the zinc bath while Grandma stood warming the big, rough towel, ready; to rub me dry. I glowered at them and grabbed the towel, covering as much as I could of myself.

"There, look what you've done, and I don't know if there's another big towel dry yet. It was raining all day yesterday," said Grandma crossly, dragging the sopping towel out of the bath. I held my head down. I simply would not get out of the bath while those two young women were there. I was too shy.

It was a sheltered life we led I suppose, and one never saw near-nudity on the sands or beaches in Swansea where we, Landore children spent those long summer holidays. Besides, I might get teased as indeed I was, soon after this. I was sent with a message to Grandma Matthews one evening and took Eira along for moral support. Grandma was out and we were at the mercy of my aunt and her companion. I knew by their expressions what they were thinking, "Let's have a bit of fun out of these little kids." And I was right, as my aunt said, "Come on you two, give us a song."

Eira and I shrank back in our chairs, but daren't disobey. I don't think Eira sang a note, but my husky voice trembled with misery as I sang 'Iesu, bugail da, o gwrando.' (Jesus, good shepherd, hear me). They screamed with laughter. How I hated their cruelty. I vowed I would never take a message to Grandma Matthews's again. Never, never.

For our chapel's annual Band of Hope concert there were weekly pratices for the cantatas we were to sing. The music was always in tonic solfa and the children were more excited about the pretty white dresses they had to wear than about the actual singing.

Not far from the chapel there was a sweet shop where the older ones bought tiny, red, crescent-shaped cachoux called 'Sweet Lips' before going into the practice. They were supposed to make your breath smell sweet and were very, very expensive. We small fry had to be content with 'Uncle Luke's', a cheap boiled sweet in every imaginable colour.

I envied the 'Sweet Lips' brigade and resolved that I would save up to buy some for myself, but I never saw them in the shops I went to. They seemed to be connected in some way with that shop near the chapel, a long way from my home, and only with the Band of Hope concert.

****

Evelyn went to the same private school as Ethel had attended. It was considered very select and none of the girls dared be seen without gloves when out of school.

One morning her teacher praised Evelyn for the neat way her gloves had been darned and gave her a good mark.

"And of course, Evelyn, you darned them yourself didn't you?" Evelyn had to admit she hadn't.

"Do you mean to tell me you let your mother do it?"

"No. It was my grandmother." This was worse still and she lost not only the good mark but two marks for letting an old lady do her darning.

****

Now began the agony of starting at my new school in Swansea. It was considered an excellent school where 'results' and good work were concerned, but I had heard grim tales about the headmistress, who was a terrifying person. Children tiptoed past her room in fear that she might appear.

Ray was in the sixth form and took me along with her on the first morning. Grandma's last words as we left the inn were:

"You look after Hannah fach, Ray. Mind now," and my cousin was as good as her word, which was a great comfort.

The school was in a very old building and an adjacent church hall was used as an extra classroom. To reach this we had to walk through a narrow, winding, white-washed passage. I found myself in a vast, draughty room which was the church hall and this was Form 1A.

That first year was sheer misery and the very thing I feared happened. I was walking along the corridor when the headmistress's door opened and an imperious voice called "Come here, girl."

Trembling, I awaited my fate.

"Take this shilling around the classes and ask if one of the teachers can change it for me." Seeing my hesitation she said sharply, "Run along, and be quick about it."

No teacher likes being disturbed when marking the register, so my appearance with the wretched shilling was unwelcome, especially as in one case I went into the same room twice, not realising that one room ran into another, separated by a glass partition. I was now in a part of the building I had never even seen and plodded on, holding the coin, only to be told with frowns or a shake of the head that no one had the change of a shilling.

Back in the playground, I knew I must face the headmistress, having failed. I had been in the school one week. Could I be expected to know where everywhere was?

Miserable, I knocked at the door and explained.

"What! Do you mean to tell me that you've been to all the classes and none of my staff has the change of a shilling?"

I nodded, handing over the shilling. Just then, a teacher I had seen only vaguely at assembly came in.

"A strange thing; none of my teachers has the change of a shilling," sneered the headmistress, and I squirmed.

Eagerly the newcomer said "I have change," and she counted out sixpence a threepenny bit and three pennies.

Looks were exchanged and four accusing eyes were fixed on my shrinking form. I wished I was dead.

"You said you had been to all the classes," the headmistress said, and at a nod from her the teacher left the room and me to my fate.

When the door had closed and we were alone again, she took a sheet of foolscap paper and wrote in large letters "I HAVE TOLD A LIE". It was viciously pinned to the wall just inside the door and I was ordered to sign my name beneath the statement. I did so and was made to stand underneath that condemning notice throughout the day for all to see who entered her room. I longed to have the courage to say, "It's not true. I thought I'd been to all the classes!"

How could I be expected to know that the building in the yard was a science classroom. Science was not for first-year pupils. Grandma was furious and demanded that my father should go to the school the following day but, after talking it over, they thought I would fare better in future if they let the matter rest.

At the first lesson in French I knew I was going to love

learning that language. My cousin Ray was able to help me, she being in her final year, and while doing my homework I was so interested that she listened while I tackled chapter after chapter in the French textbook. At the end of a French lesson I couldn't resist telling the teacher how far I had gone in the book. She half-smiled and said, "Well now, do you think you are getting on well in French?" I beamed at these words.

"Or do you think you are a very clever girl?"

Such sarcasm from a teacher is hardly encouraging for a pupil.

When Grandma first heard me reading French, she looked at my book and remarked, "Fancy that. French people having the same words as we have in Wales," pointing to the words 'pont' and 'fenetre'.

She read them as they would read in Welsh, as indeed 'pont' is Welsh for 'bridge' as it is in French, and the French 'fenetre' is similar to the Welsh word 'fenestr' for 'window'. When I explained how the French pronounced it, she would not have it, saying "Ridiculous, calling it 'pong' instead of 'pont'," stressing the 'T' at the end. But her interest grew as she learned more French words that resembled the Welsh ones.

****

Dick now started at the Boys' school in Swansea, so we travelled together by train. There were two ways of getting to my school. You could walk down High Street, slip up a short lane and in a few minutes you were at the school. This was the quicker and most popular way, but I was to go with Dick the longer way, along Alexandra Road, after a distressing experience I had when taking the short way one Monday morning.

Outside the Mackworth restaurant I had seen a queue of poorly dressed children waiting for the doors to open. Assistants then came out and gave them bags of stale buns and cakes left over from the Saturday. These the children munched as they slunk off to their homes, somewhere behind High Street. I did not take that route on Monday mornings again.

****

I discovered that I had a cousin who was also in her first year at my school. Why hadn't I met her? I wanted to know. Grandma then explained that she was a daughter of my father's sister Annie, who lived in Swansea. This sounded very mysterious until she said that this sister had been brought up, not by Grandma Matthews, but by Grandma Matthews's mother, so that there hadn't been the 'togetherness' of all children living with their parents. It was quite common in large Welsh families for one child to be taken into the grandparents' home. I know of several cases where this had happened, no doubt to ease the parents' burden. I had met Auntie Annie a few times when she visited Grandma Matthews, but none of her children were known to me.

"When you get to school, find out which class she is in and make yourself known to her. She is your first cousin, remember."

The family assumed that we would naturally become friends, but to me it was a problem. Where, in this crowded playground, would I find this unknown cousin?

I tried asking girls in other first-year classes, but they couldn't tell me. Anyway, it was playtime and they wanted to make the most of it. Perhaps my timorous manner was too half-hearted.

How I envied the two most popular girls in the sixth form! As soon as they appeared in the playground they were surrounded by admiring 'fans'. One girl was very fair, the other dark with projecting teeth. I wished I had projecting teeth and brown eyes. I thought they were as beautiful as film stars.

"Well Doris" demanded my father, "have you spoken to your cousin Muriel yet?" I had to confess my failure which they could not understand, and as the term went by my efforts faded. There were three Form Ones, A, B and C. I was in 1A.

School continued to be a trial, especially P.T. which exhausted me so that when I reached home I didn't want to do anything but lie down. I daren't tell Grandma that one reason for my feeling so wretched was the pain I felt when I had to vault the horse. I knew it was the result of my jumping off the old bone-shaker of a bike in our yard and landing on the leatherless saddle. My mother wrote a letter to the headmistress asking if I might miss P.T. as I was anaemic and found it exhausting.

"Certainly not. You look as if you could do with some exercise," I was told and the P.T. lessons continued, though my teacher excused me the horse-vaulting, and P.T. became more bearable.

It was a shock when I came home from school one day to find Grandma Matthews sitting sadly in our kitchen. My cousin Muriel had died, a little girl of about thirteen, or possibly less. The child I hadn't bothered to make friends with! I had been beastly and both Grandmas thought I simply hadn't cared enough to get to know her. How could I have been so horrible to my little cousin? My suffering over that stands out among my memories of my schooldays. What my parents didn't know was, God forgive me, that I *had* seen a little girl like myself whom I hesitated to approach, a nondescript, timid little girl. Had she been jolly and popular like the two film-stars I so admired, would I have hesitated? I'm sure I wouldn't. I tried to tell myself, "She should have tried to find me."

CHAPTER THIRTEEN

The shopping days with Grandma were over for me and it was fun to go into town on Saturday afternoons, a whole crowd of us, to the High Street Picture House. Here they gave free ices to the patrons during the performance. In we'd march, wearing our school blazers and straw hats which were our vouchers for going in at half-price. The usherettes served each of us with an ice which we ate and then in the dark, while they went for more ice cream, we crept down to the rows in front and were given a second lot: that is until a wary usherette recognised some of us and that put an end to that bit of sharp practice.

We spent the lunch hour, after eating our sandwiches, in wandering round Woolworth's where we would stand for ages at the book counter, reading the meaning of our dreams in a dream book.

"Keep your inky fingers off those books! You kids never buy a copy, but I bet you've read every word," the assistant said, which was perfectly true. I found the dream book in Woolworth's much easier to read than Grandma's big, black, oil-cloth covered one, all in Welsh, with "Breuddwydion" (Dreams) in white letters on the cover.

We practised a little blackmail on this girl as the result of an incident we had witnessed one dinner-hour. It was about one-thirty, when there were few shoppers about. As we entered the store we saw a tramp at the jewellery counter, stuffing his pockets with rings and watches. Not a sign of an assistant anywhere: they were in a group at the far end of the shop having a gossip, our dream-book girl among them.

Gwyneth and I just stood, watching all this, helpless. Then the manager appeared, shouted at the girls and, grabbing the thief, roughly emptied his pockets of the jewellery and shoved him out of the shop.

"Come to my office, all of you there,"he called to the group of assistants, but our girl, whose counter was at the back, escaped his sharp eyes and slipped back to her place. But we had seen her there with the others. This was a golden opportunity. Coolly we walked up to her counter and started reading, knowing we could tell the 'boss' if we liked; and the books became tattier and tattier.

The local Art Gallery was another favourite haunt on wet days, especially the china room. Swansea china had a particular interest for us as pottery had been a flourishing industry in Swansea. Many homes had pieces of Swansea pottery, the owners not realising how valuable it would become. There were girls in my class from an area known as 'The Patri', a corruption I expect from the word 'pottery'. There were cases of Nantgarw ware in the china room which must have impressed Gwyneth.

She was a year younger than me and school became more bearable after her arrival as she was a real 'card'. One day she told me, giggling, that a woman I didn't know had seen us together and asked Gwyneth who I was, saying, "She looks as if she's somebody. You know, classy like."

"Oh yes," said the wily Gwyneth, remembering our recent hour in the Art Gallery, "She's really related to,"(here she had to think quickly) "Lady Nantgarw: but its a secret."

This worried me as I had visions of ending up in prison, and when at home I asked, "Grandma, who is Lady Nantgarw?"

"I've never heard of such as person. Why?"

"Oh, nothing. Only because I saw some china in the Art Gallery with Nantgarw on it."

"Well, I'm glad you go to the Art Gallery instead of worrying those poor girls in Woolworth's like I've been told you and Gwyneth have been doing."

Another day while wandering through one of the rooms in the Art Gallery I noticed one small picture covered by a velvet curtain. Never able to resist peeping behind curtains, I drew it back to reveal a delicate water-colour of a beautiful city. During one of the headmistress's dreaded English lessons, she asked which of us ever visited the Art Gallery. A few hands went up.

"Well, who can tell me the name of the picture that is covered by a velvet curtain?" Her expression was cynical and I hesitated, hoping my memory served me right before I put up my hand.

"Orleans Cathedral," I said, thankful that no one was able to deny this. She simply nodded. It was too much to expect a word of praise from her.

The time came when it was impossible to escape from her vigilance. In my form, 4A, there was a glass-fronted case with a skeleton, upright in it. This faced us all day, which was not pleasant. Worse still, next to the case was a door, also glass-fronted, into the headmistress's room, so she kept a constant eye on us. I adored the English teacher in this form but, owing to our habit of giggling, Gwyneth was put to sit several desks away from mine. It was poetry reading, which I loved, and when I was told to read part of a poem the words 'dew-drops glistening' struck me as very amusing, as they so aptly described the perpetual dew-drop that hung from the science mistress's nose. I caught Gwyneth's eye and we both burst out laughing. Through her 'spying door' stormed the headmistress and as we dare not explain our behaviour we were punished. I suffered from my teacher's unbelieving expression, as I had let her down. I had up until that moment been enjoying the lesson so much.

Reading was my great joy, I couldn't get enough books to satisfy me. When I read in one of the 'Dainty Novels' Gwyneth liked to buy that the heroine was pale like me, and 'The pallor of her face was not the pallor of ill-health, but of refinement' I found it reassuring. Perhaps, as the woman had said to Gwyneth, I did have a 'classy' look about me. And on Sunday evenings, when the documents of the Estate were being read aloud, I felt proud to belong to Grandma's family. Although we now lived in a public house, one day we might live in a castle.

This snobbish attitude was belied one evening when I promised a girl in the playground that I would go up to her street to play with her after tea. It was some distance away from The Station Inn and the people of the area were strangers to me, except for the girl in my class. We chased each other and knocked at doors and ran away, huddling together in a doorway nearby to watch the owners opening the door, look round to see who had been knocking and shut the door again. We laughed as we waited, but I was conscious of the smell of sweaty clothes and unwashed bodies and knew I should be at home or in Eira's, where Grandma thought I was. My guilty look gave me away as I entered our kitchen and when I admitted I hadn't after all, been in Eira's, and mentioned the name of the street, my father was very cross.

"What on earth made you go there to play? I know that street. They're a dirty lot. When I go there for the insurance the smell comes out to meet you in the passage." I didn't want to go again.

****

Once a week our English lesson was taken by the headmistress. She would spring on us a subject about which we had to write an essay. There was a choice of one of three. They were:

'America', about which I knew nothing except that two of my father's uncles lived there: So that was out.

'Fairies', which sounded rather childish.

'The history of the English theatre' about which I knew a little, and therefore was the one I chose. The following week came the results. The headmistress sat in the teacher's desk and asked,

"Who can tell me the meaning of the word 'histrionic'?" I waited, butterflies in my stomach as I remembered I had used it in my essay. I looked round. Not a hand went up. At last I put mine up.

"Not you," said the headmistress, waving my hand aside, "I know that you know it." She didn't praise me or my essay, but she flayed the others with biting sarcasm.

The following week, instead of an essay, we were asked what literature our parents read at home.

I said, "My Grandma reads the bible and "The Sunday Companion" and my mother reads the New Testament and 'The Sunday Companion'."

"Anything else?" and my face burned as I added "Silas and Joseph Hocking books."

"And your father. What does he read?"

"John Bull and 'Titbits'."

I was devoured with shame at the poor taste of my parents and Grandma's, but comforted as I listened to the other girls, whose parents were equally uncultured it seemed.

The Free Library was somewhere to spend half an hour at lunch time, where we could look through the expensive magazines we never saw at home. We called there, too, on the way home to borrow books. One day Elsie, one of my friends asked Gwyneth and me to go there for a book for her mother and to the Home and Colonial Store. Her mother had made two lists, one for the food and the other of book titles. We managed to behave without giggling in the library until Elsie handed a list to the severe old gentleman who read aloud,

"Kippers? We haven't a book of that name. Do you mean 'Kipps' by H.G. Wells?" Elsie didn't know.

"Margarine?"

Realising we had given him the wrong list she hastily found the other. We exploded with laughter as soon as we reached the corridor outside.

I started my romantic reading with Zane Grey and 'Riders of the Purple Sage'. The very title was colourful. A customer seeing the book lying around in the middle kitchen where I'd left it on the window sill, asked my father if he might borrow it. This started a friendship between him and his wife and myself. I don't remember if either was attractive or not, but only that I was intrigued by their living room. Always excited by curtains and what they might conceal, I noticed a floral-patterned one covering what turned out to be a kind of open cupboard in which were kept cups and saucers and on one shelf a few books. It was made out of an orange box with shelves fixed in it. When I commented on the originality of the idea the wife looked embarrassed. I was sorry, but I had never seen furniture in friends' homes, except that which was like our own: a dresser, grandfather clock, cupboards and book cases.

One evening I was about to call there with a new book to lend them when my cousin Claudia stopped me and suggested that it would be better if I did not go there so often.

"Why?" I asked, in innocent surprise.

"Because she says you are 'after' her husband."

I burst out laughing. The idea was so ridiculous, and I went home. Grandma looked serious for a moment and then said:

"I think Claudia is right. Don't bother with them. They are

not our sort. They don't go to chapel, do they? Off to the sands every Sunday with a basket of food, if you please. Leave them be, Hannah fach."

I wasn't upset. This incident gave me a few moments of disappointment and surprise. These people didn't matter to me, apart from exchanging books. Was he an attractive man? I had no idea what colour his eyes were even. There was a tinge of feeling unjustly hurt, but I quickly forgot the whole thing.

****

When I reached the sixth form I made a new friend, Enid. She told me she had a cousin who had actually written a book of poems. His name was Iolo Williams and he was descended from the eminent Welsh poet Iolo Morgannwg (Iolo of Glamorgan). Grandma was interested in this news, especially when my father said that Iolo Morgannwg was really the bardic name for Iolo Williams. My respect for Enid and her cousin grew by the minute, as he hunted through an old 'History of Wales'.

"Here you are then,"he said triumphantly. "Listen to this bit; 'Iolo Morgannwg or Iolo Williams lived for some time," my father paused and slyly watched my face as he read slowly, stressing each word, "at Boverton Castle in the Vale of Glamorgan." I almost leaped from excitement. Here we were, back again to our romantic castle and the Estate.

"Why did he live there?" I demanded. "Was he related to our family?" My words were tumbling over each other. If that was the case it was almost as wonderful to be related to such a famous poet as to be connected with the castle. "Perhaps that is why I am so fond of poetry," I said.

"We are all poets in Wales,"my father said drily. "Look at your Uncle Walter. He is a past master of the 'Englyn'." (This is a form of Welsh verse). That he was of Grandma's family was unarguable. I was delighted to tell Enid all we had discovered.

****

A girl in my form told me she was going to a palmist to have her hands read. This was enough for me to go along too. I was told that I could earn my living in three different ways. I could become a nurse, which I was sure I could never be as I dreaded even wiping blood off Dick's hand when he fell down. Touching the cut, I felt the pain right through my own hand. Then the palmist said I could go on the stage. That was a laugh as I was too shy to stand up in class and answer my teacher. Then, continued the palmist, I might become a teacher, which proved an accurate prophesy, and she was not far out mentioning acting. I was to realise later that as a teacher you have to be something of an actress as I discovered when telling my little ones a story. If it was very sad, their eyes would grow rounder, their little mouths tremble and I knew at that moment it was time to switch off acting so realistically and bring in a touch of fun to the story.

It happened that at school all the girls who seemed to have enough brains to do well in the important exams went in for teaching automatically. I remember the day when every girl in my form was asked if she intended applying for Training College or University. One girl who seemed much cleverer than any of us said she didn't intend applying. Like a dog worrying a bone, the headmistress demanded to know the reason and was told that the family couldn't afford it. One glance at her clothing should have revealed that, and we were all sorry for her obvious distress as she gave the reason.

I had been disappointed at the visit to the palmist since she had said nothing about Grandma and the estate, as surely that should have appeared in the reading of my hands! Nor was there any handsome young man who would adore me. My friend and I both took a dim view of the palmist's powers.

Quite soon after this Eira and I heard about Miss Jones, a fortune-teller who, so people said, was 'very good' at it. So up we went one dark evening to this grubby little house, a long way from where we lived. We found the house easily enough as we had been told to look for a house with a card in the window reading 'Dressmaker'. A wispy-haired woman opened the door furtively and drew us inside, where we joined several young women in the parlour; a dreary room where the horse-hair sofa cut into the backs of my legs unmercifully. On a chair in a dim corner sat a woman who looked much older than my mother. What fortune was there for her, I wondered? There was no sign of a magazine or anything else to read while Eira was having her fortune told, so I looked round the darkening room: a heavy chest of drawers with bits of china and a glass case with a stuffed bird in it was the only item of furniture of interest.

My turn came at long last. Madam Sarita, a name she had concocted from her two names Sarah Marguerita I understood, was a frowsy fat woman who held a dirty pack of cards as she sat at the kitchen table. On a piece of blue velvet rested a crystal ball. I shuffled the cards inexpertly, as all I could play was 'Beggar your Neighbour' and chose twenty-one which the palmist arranged face downwards in some secret order.

Then she droned on about my having to look after my health. But my eyes were drawn to the wall behind her where, hanging on a coat-hanger from the picture rail was a grubby off-white cotton or calico nightdress. Seeing my interest, she explained that this was to have been her wedding nightgown. The villain had jilted her at the altar. It had hung there ever since. Many years I thought, by the state of it. I suppose it was a kind of warning to young girls not to trust men.

"I see a man suffering from his chest. Is that your father? No, don't tell me; I'm supposed to tell you, my girl." So I didn't mention that he suffered from asthma.

If I wanted the crystal reading it would cost another half crown. I decided it wasn't worth it, but what she told me gave me happy dreams for a long time.

People went to Madam Sarita from far and near and the story of her wedding nightgown was well known. When a relative of mine went to see her, Madam Sarita advised her to put her affairs in order, though all she wanted to know was if her sister would ever marry. Soon after this my relative died and her sister married the widower. So Madam Sarita was right in that event.

CHAPTER 14

At the end of term, during my final year at school, a concert was arranged and as one of my friends, Maria, was a good singer, she was asked to give a solo and I was to accompany her, my piano playing having improved. I was able to sight-read pretty well, so the question of choosing a song arose. Naturally romantic, we chose 'The Sunshine of your Smile' and practised and practised until a few days before the concert. When our teacher asked us which song she was to sing, Maria produced what we thought was a lovely ballad, and we were really crestfallen when the teacher said it was most unsuitable for a song to be sung at a school concert.

All that practising! and how I had admired the ease with which my friend reached the high notes with her rich voice, and now everything must be sacrificed for whatever stodgy song the teacher chose from The National Song Book! I think it was either 'The Ash Grove' or 'The Minstrel Boy' that was selected, but whatever it was it certainly wasn't as charming in our opinion as 'The Sunshine of your Smile'. We decided that the teacher was much too old to appreciate such a tender love-song. She was surely about thirty.

It was the custom at our school to celebrate Empire Day by gathering round the Union Jack in the playground and singing a few patriotic songs, including 'Rule Britannia' of course. There we were, enthusiastically extolling the British Empire, singing lustily, when the headmistress appeared. A ricketty set of iron steps ran from the playground to a small building where cookery classes were held. She walked half way up these steps, stopped, turned to face us and held up her hand. The singing petered out half way through a chorus and we looked at her, wondering what was wrong. Then followed an amazing speech in which she told us that to extol the virtues of the British Empire was wrong. We learned of all the bad things that had been done in the name of patriotism towards the native populations. Then we scattered lamely about the playground.

****

The privations of war came right into our classroom the day the whole school was gathered together by the headmistress. Partitions were folded back to allow room for all to hear the dire news. We were told there were people in France who were hungry and that we in Britain must tighten our belts and be willing to forego luxuries if we wished to help the war effort.

It was our duty to go without unnecessary food such as sweets, chocolate, pastries and ice-cream, she said. She wasn't commanding us to be sternly unselfish, but if we looked at the notice board in the main corridor we would see a sheet of foolscap pinned thereon where any pupils who cared enough for their country's welfare might sign. This would be a positive gesture of the genuineness of the school's patriotism. That appeal sent us in a solid if reluctant procession to the corridor where not one sheet of foolscap, but three, were pinned. Each bore the statement:

'I promise not to buy sweets, chocolates, pastries or ice cream until the war is over,' followed by a blank space for signatures.

I think most of my form signed and faced the miserable prospect ahead. It was horrid having to watch Dick eating his sweets and Evelyn tucking into chocolates while I had to be patriotic and refuse. This misery was aggravated when a big box of chocolates came for me from a chocolate firm in return for twenty wrappers from tins of cocoa. Nobly, I gave it to Dick. He had no scruples about accepting it. His headmaster had not asked any such sacrifice of his boys.

When I told my fellow sufferer, Gwyneth, who had also signed, she surprised me by saying that I was silly to have given the chocolates away, pointing out that what we had signed was a vow not to BUY any sweets, chocolates, pastries and ice-cream. We hadn't sworn not to EAT them. I was tempted to ask Dick to give the box back, but he had already eaten most of the chocolates.

I found them doubly delicious after those months, which seemed like years, since I had tasted them.

We heard no more about the foolscap affair from the headmistress.

****

The scholars who showed promise in art were given extra art lessons at the Art School in Swansea on Saturdays. I enjoyed these until the day I became disgusted with the art master's treatment of the owl I had painted. I had thought it quite good and was alarmed when he dipped my brush in the pot of dirty water I was using for rinsing it. When I pointed this out to him, thinking he had made a mistake, he took no notice but calmly washed the whole bird with the dirty water. To my surprise the too vivid colours I had used had now been toned down beautifully with excellent effect. He grinned as I thanked him for teaching me something more about painting.

But when the lessons in drawing from live models began I nearly fainted from shock. A young woman wearing a dressing gown came into the classroom, stepped up on to the dais, dropped her robe and sat down on a chair in an artistic pose. And there she sat waiting for us to draw her while we looked at her, both boys and girls of about my age, in all her nakedness. I didn't even attempt to make a rough sketch of her. The bold woman, I thought. What would Grandma have said if she knew?

There and then I decided to give up art lessons.

****

Our clubroom at The Station Inn was very popular with our young friends as we were allowed to play there, except on Forester Club nights. In the morning it was given a thorough cleaning and we weren't allowed to play there during that afternoon. It was a splendid place for acting the plays which I wrote and directed, and in which I played leading lady, a privilege I firmly demanded as the daughter of the house. The plots were taken from films we had seen; cowboys and Indians in every one of them. I took the part of Mabel Normand, the star of many films at that time and by bringing my curls forward on to my forehead and tying a ribbon round my head to keep them in place, gave a fair imitation of the hairstyle she wore. Dick brought his friends along, so we had plenty of cowboys and Indians. Dick was a bit of a nuisance, insisting for some reason on being Lord Kitchener in every play, seated on an armchair as a throne, or brandishing a sword (one of my father's walking sticks) and every now and then leaping up in warlike attitude and laying about him in fury. So, Lord Kitchener appeared in every play we did.

"Where are you going with my darning wool?" Grandma demanded suspiciously one wet Saturday afternoon.

"It's only for a game we are playing," I replied, not daring to mention the word 'play' which suggested the theatre. Games were all right though, but she didn't trust me.

"And what do you want that bar of soap for?"

"To make a Charlie Chaplin moustache for Dick's pal. The soap's to make it stick on," I explained innocently.

She was astonished when she appeared at the clubroom door to see us all dressed up in play costumes and making an ear-splitting noise.

"What are you supposed to be then? All dressed up like Rebecca Rioters!" Reassured that we were behaving ourselves she left us alone, but that night I asked her who the Rebecca Rioters were. She described how a band of men, mainly farmers, objecting strongly to the turnpike gates at which a toll had to be paid, demolished the gates and threw them into the sea in Swansea. These men were dressed as women so that they wouldn't be recognised by the authorities and the police.

"Why were these men called Rebecca's Daughters?" I wanted to know.

"You open the bible, Hannah fach, and find Genesis; its in

there somewhere."

Reluctantly I fumbled through the chapters, looking for the name Rebecca.

"Here, give it to me," and Grandma searched while I wondered what on earth this had to do with our dressing up.

"Now then, listen to this. It's chapter twenty-four, 'And they blessed Rebecca and said unto her, Thou art our sister, be thou the mother of thousands and millions and let thy seed possess the gate of those which hate them.'"

I read for myself, remarking "It's spelt Rebekah in the bible though."

"Never mind about that," Grandma said. "I noticed that you were wearing the curtains from the cupboard round you. I hope you haven't left the clubroom 'sang de vang'." 'Sang de vang' is an expression used in Wales to signify a disordered state.

It was in our clubroom plays that I experienced my first 'falling in love'. The hero was one of Dick's friends of my own age. I don't remember if he was good-looking or not: it didn't seem to matter. I was in love with the idea of 'Love' as seen on the Pictures. He liked me, too, and in my mind I built it up for all I was worth into my first real romance, perhaps encouraged by his proximity as I fixed the black wool moustache on his upper lip. Another of Dick's friends liked me too and when we started meeting for a walk in the summer evenings I had two swains. We would stroll along, me in the middle, sedately enough, but I soon became fed up with this. In the winter this feeling of frustration was aggravated by my feeling the cold, although the 'love of my life' used to take my hand and place it in his jacket or blazer pocket. He would squeeze it until we came to a lamp post, when it was wise to break away. I wasn't in the least aware of the other boy's attractive, rich speaking voice which was musical, or of anything other than that he was a nuisance, and one evening I made it plain that I wasn't meeting him again. After that, it was me and my beloved. It was the easiest thing in the world, when fixing his moustache, to slip a little billet-doux into his pocket, probably some romantic line of poetry I had read. I don't recall having many from him though: it was a very one-sided affair really. There must be more to this 'being in love', I thought, and I invented a clever secret code for us. A code was more in keeping with romance than an ordinary letter.

Here it is.

As I worked out my message, I felt gloriously guilty. It might take me ages and in the end ran, 'See you tonight'. I sent him many such messages and awaited his replies, which were few. I expect he found them difficult, possibly silly, but whatever they were they thrilled me to receive them.

Later on I wondered what on earth I saw in him to make me take such pains, and I easily forgot him.

****

Evelyn had what her tailor called a perfect figure and when I had grown too big to sleep in Grandma's bed, Evelyn and I shared the front bedroom. I noticed that though she had a fine bust, she was considerably flattened by the brassieres she made. It was simply a wide strip of strong cotton material with hooks on one end and eyes on the other to fasten it under one armpit. Straps of ribbon were sewn on, and there was her brassiere. So it was natural that when I felt it was time I wore one I made one exactly the same, which boyishly flattened my bust. We both made several and it was years before I noticed that the ones you could buy in the drapers' weren't shaped at all like ours: in fact they emphasised the bust. I wouldn't buy one, as I was shy of having a bust anyway and had got into the habit of sitting with round shoulders to hide my developing figure. To me this had nothing to do with romance which was all dreamy, romantic adoration of facial beauty and love of the aesthetic.

****

CODE FOR MY LOVE LETTERS

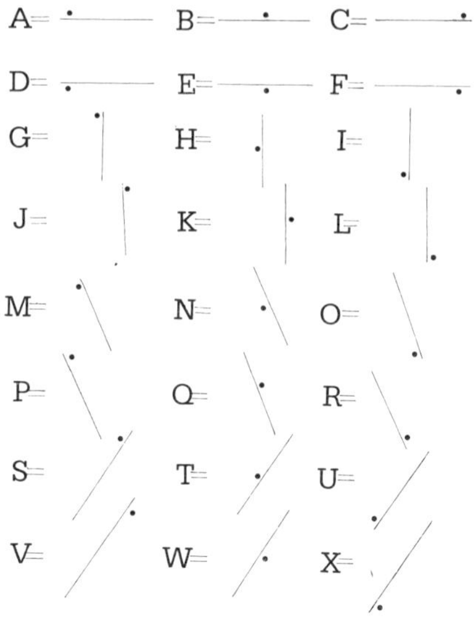

y = y   z = z

One day I saw in the newsagent's a magazine new to me called 'The Magnet'. I bought it, attracted by the cover which showed schoolboys wearing toppers and tail-coats and 'bumfreezers'. Zane Grey was dropped flat and I couldn't get enough stories of those public school boys and I grew to know Harry Wharton and his chums better than Dick's friends. Soon I discovered 'The Gem' and Tom Merry. How lovely, to live in a beautiful school like 'Greyfriars' or 'St. Jim's' and to be able to have your own study for feeds, and a school tuckshop. I was delighted to introduce them to Dick, who enjoyed them too, and we talked about their adventures endlessly, to Grandma's disgust. All books except those with religious themes were wicked. They had to be hidden, and where better than in the parlour where a wicker easy chair with a deep chintz frill hung to the floor? The cross-piece of wood underneath neatly hid a pile of these weeklies and, with the excuse of practising the piano and the pages turned over with one hand, and just about any notes played with the other sounded all right. I got away with this until the cleaning woman found the weeklies and they were confiscated. But that wasn't the end of it. Dick had accidentally left a 'Magnet' around and Grandma found it, read it all through and, to our amazement, enjoyed it! After that we were allowed to read 'The Magnet' and 'Gem'. She would ask every week.

"What has Billy Bunter been up to today?" or

"What happened to that horrid boy who cheated Tom Merry last week?"

****

The only time I didn't like going into the clubroom was during one summer holiday. On the last day of term our maths. teacher, a stickler for work, made me promise to swot for an hour every day of the long holiday. What a penance for simply forgetting to give the answer to a problem in pounds, shillings and pence! I had given the answer in shillings. But she was like that. She gave me nine per cent for geometry because I spelt 'chord' as 'cord' and 'arc' as 'ark', even though I had worked out the sums correctly. An important exam. was looming and she told me that I was much too careless to pass. Grandma was furious and insisted that my mother take me to see my Sunday School teacher, Miss Blodwen Morgan, who was also a school teacher. In her parlour, bless her, we spent several evenings over my homework. She thought that as long as I had my answers right, no examiner would just give me 'nought' for having one spelling error. So I defied my enemy, and mentally putting out my tongue at her, passed.

To my relief, in the next class we had an utterly different teacher, both in appearance and attitude. Although I was sometimes careless she gave me credit for working out problems correctly. But the great moment came at the end of my first term when I scored ninety-five per cent in arithmetic. So I proved I wasn't the duffer my previous teacher had made me out to be.

"Did you go and tell that nasty old teacher you used to have that you were top in your sums?" Grandma asked.

"I wouldn't dare," I replied, remembering the misery of Monday mornings in her class. The sight of her standing there in black high-necked blouse, long black skirt covered by a black sateen apron, holding an enormous pair of compasses in her right hand, ready for the fray, was too forbidding.

"Who will come out and do Theorem Five on the board?" As if eager I'd put up my hand, praying she would think I must know it. This usually worked, because then she would not ask me to explain the theorem.

Although happy in having a kinder maths. teacher, when I passed into a higher class I lost contact with my adored English teacher, Miss Lord. I flung myself into reading poetry without guidance. I didn't like the new English teacher. Grandma wasn't at all interested in English literature and my parents were too busy running the inn. In my dreams I was going to become a poet, not using my real name, of course. I would be Terry Luvelle, the name I made up when the 'actress' phase ruled.

For the doggerel I wrote for the school magazine I used my own name, my pseudonym was to be kept for the day when I wrote wonderful romances and real poetry. But I composed poetic-sounding lines like 'Your eyes are like wet blackberries'. It didn't matter that my Charlie Chaplin-moustached boy friend had nondescript hazel eyes. They had given me a line of poetry.

On my birthday Miss Blodwen Morgan who had, by coaching me, restored my faith in teachers, gave me a copy of the New Testament. On the inside of the cover she had written 'For God so loved Doris Matthews that He gave His only-begotten Son.' The family were delighted, especially Grandma, but I confess to a feeling of embarrassment when friends opened this present from my Sunday School teacher. They read: then looked at me as surprised as if I had suddenly sprouted a Salvation Army bonnet on my head.

Many years later when my home was partially destroyed by fire (The Kingsbridge Inn where my mother had spent her childhood), all the upstairs was burnt out. There were so many of the books I had loved and all were lost in that fire.

Picture postcards of the front of the inn, which showed my twenty-first birthday gift, a piano, stuck half way in and out of the upstairs lounge window, sold in the local stationer's like hot cakes.

CHAPTER FIFTEEN

The idea of boys having studies of their own, where they could entertain friends, gave Dick and me the urge to have a study. We chose Grandma's bedroom for this, using the chest of drawers as a food safe and smuggling cups of milk and Welsh cakes upstairs. It wasn't much fun sitting on the feather bed, balancing cup and plate on this sloppy table top, but we tried to enjoy it and were not really sorry when Grandma came upstairs and caught us. That this was our study, just like the boys in the 'Gem' had no effect on her.

"Food in my bedroom? What next? You'll draw mice up here that's what you'll do. Come downstairs and bring all that stuff with you." Miserably we carried the dishes to the kitchen, where my mother wasn't intrigued by the idea either.

Uncle Alf understood though, and told us about the days when he was at boarding school. One of the boys was a day boy whose father kept the grocer shop which supplied the school. His name was Mason and the boys used to shout after him as he went home from school,

"Mason, Mason, rotten eggs and frowsty bacon." It sounded cruel but the story eased the unpleasantness of our being caught.

****

Eira and I spent hours playing duets on the piano in her parlour and one summer evening we were interrupted by her brother David, who was in his twenties, and his friend Idwal. They wanted a private chat so we were sent into the kitchen where we waited hoping they would leave soon. The windows were open and their voices, annoyingly indistinct, went on and on. The words of their conversation made us listen hard. Idwal was saying "I'm sure she puts Dragon's blood in my tea, David."

'Dragon's blood!' Immediately we were mystified and excited. By now the young man's voice was raised to a frenzy as he continued, "I'll never get over Ann letting me down as she did. Eloping with that visiting preacher fellow. Never. I'll love her till I die."

I looked questioningly at Eira who nodded as David was saying, "Why then are you going to the Jenkinses so often? It's Megan you're after, isn't it?"

Eira whispered. "She's Shirley's big sister. You know her."

As the parlour door was being opened the voices became louder, "Why do I go there? I don't know, David. I don't *want* her yet some how I feel I'm being dragged there, night after night. Megan Jenkins is determined to get me to marry her and I've been told she's put Dragon's blood in my tea." They were talking as they walked along the passage on their way out.

Eagerly Eira and I went into the parlour and closed the door, but we didn't feel like playing the piano any more that evening: the strange potion, Dragon's blood, filled our imagination, and we talked of nothing else.

What was it and how did it work? That we *must* find out by keeping a watchful eye on Idwal's frequent visits to Shirley's house across the road from Eira's shop. It didn't occur to us to look in the dictionary, but I did ask Grandma innocently enough. Her reply was "Dragon's blood? *I've* never heard of it. Such nonsense. Reading too many books, that's what you're doing, merch i."

Within months Idwal and Megan were married in the chapel and vanished from our lives as they moved to London where Idwal had gained a teaching post. But the charm must have worked as, according to Shirley who spent several holidays at their home, it was a very happy marriage.

Eira and I agreed it was very disappointing as Idwal had sworn to love his false Ann for ever and ever. We decided to find out if, by any remote possibility, the words 'Dragon's blood' would be in my dictionary. Yes, they were. To our dismay the dictionary said,

'A resinous exudation from the scaly fruits of a climbing palm: a native of Borneo. When powdered is carmine red in colour, used for colouring wood, etc."

What a let down. Yet it must have been known as an aphrodisiac in those days. The very words sounded romantic and thrilling to our young minds and we were unwilling to accept the mundane description given in the dictionary.

****

My romantic mind was disturbed at this time by Uncle Alf. By this time he had become one of the family, a wonderful help in the bar and the kitchen. He was, to me the gentle giant who had inspired me to yearn for foreign places.

I was wrestling with contours one evening when he leaned over me and asked if I needed help. It was a warm evening and I was wearing a thin, V-ncked dress which was certainly not revealing, when I felt his hand slip over my shoulder and slowly down over my breast. Then suddenly he went out of the room, relieving my momentary distress. I began to wonder about Uncle Alf. I knew he had never married and as he was a bachelor I didn't connect him with women until I overheard him talking to a customer.

"Haven't you ever had a woman?" he was asking the man. "There was a fine woman in Singapore. Whenever I was on leave there, I was her only man," continued Uncle Alf.

I shrugged it off. I just didn't want to know. Let him remain what I wanted him to be. There was no repetition of the unpleasant incident of the 'contours'.

A further hint of sex came in the form of a girl in my class. She was thin with knock-knees and, coming from somewhere in England used to say, to our amusement 'room' to rhyme with 'book' in the centre vowels. One day she told us she had peeped in her parents' bedroom and seen them in a suggestive position on the bed. We waited to see if her mother became pregnant. Her mother worked in their shop and Gwyneth and I made every excuse for buying things we didn't really need, so as to report developments. The months went by and nothing happened. We were baffled as the woman kept her slim figure and our interest flagged. We decided that this rather indecent incident witnessed by her inquisitive daughter had nothing to do with love or romance, just marriage.

****

Toothache plagued my schooldays, brought on no doubt by the iron medicine I was forever having to take. They hadn't thought of taking it through a straw then, so my visits to the dentist were frequent. It was always Grandma who took me to Mr. Scott's in Swansea where I was given gas, so I didn't mind at all. When I was old enough to go alone, I found he chattered away all the time, asking me how Grandma was. I was utterly unable to reply with the gag in my mouth. My mother said he did this to keep my mind off the filling he was doing by injection. I decided I would have no more fillings and when a filling did come out I tried being my own dentist. Someone at school told me you could do your own filling. My cavity was aching terribly, but unknown to Grandma I bought a stick of something like putty about the size of a matchstick and gave a whole Saturday afternoon to doing the job. I washed the cavity out thoroughly then melted the putty in the flame of a candle until it was soft. With a large pin I took some from the top and plugged it hard into the cavity. I lay down on my bed waiting for it to set and suffering agony for a least an hour. But it did the trick, that is until it became unstuck. When Grandma noticed me refusing my favourite sweets, she insisted on looking at my teeth and promptly took me along to Mr. Scott for a proper filling. He later took the tooth out, together with two others. This meant having a plate with three teeth, right in front.

****

Although Grandma's brother William Pryce had died, she loved visiting Capel Hendre to see her nephews and nieces. On one occasion she took Dick and me along: it was especially to talk to her nephew William, who was now the one considered the heir to the Estate. He lived on a farm a few miles from Capel Hendre. This was a real treat for us as it was such a change from Landore and its smoke.

While Grandma and Uncle William went indoors, no doubt to discuss the latest developments regarding the estate, we were sent to the orchard where we were told we might pick as many apples as we liked to take home with us, all except the ones on a particular tree, which Uncle impressed on us were to be shown at an agricultural show. What a thrill to actually pick apples from a growing tree!

To my dismay, Dick climbed the forbidden tree and cupping the rosiest apple in his hands took a large bite out of it and clambered down, leaving the mutilated apple still on its branch. How could we face Uncle William? Slowly we walked into the farmhouse on hearing him call us to have tea.

"Uncle didn't say not to bite the apples on that tree," Dick argued. "He only said we were not to pick them." He was quick to explain this and it made Grandma cross, but Uncle William thought it very clever reasoning, and Dick was invited to spend a holiday at the farm later.

After tea we were taken in the trap to 'Bronhaul', where I used to spend my holidays at Uncle Isaac's and Auntie Rachel's, with their many children. Of the four uncles it was Uncle Isaac who was best informed about the Estate. He was full of enthusiasm and determination that the Pryce family should inherit what was considered their right.

All the Pryce children and myself were gathered by him into the kitchen of 'Bronhaul' where we were made to listen attentively to something very important we should know. We listened.

"See these veins," he said dramatically, tracing them with a coal-ingrained finger slowly up his arm from the wrist. Then, seizing my arm, dragging the sleeve back to the elbow, he gently moved his finger along a vein and declared, gripping my wrist, "Remember, all of you, we haven't much money and have to work very hard to earn it, but there is blue blood running through these veins of ours."

Then having made his point, he pulled my sleeve down and fumblingly fastened the cuff-button. The idea of having blue blood was comical to us and I vaguely thought it had something to do with the blue pit-marks on Uncle's face.

On our return to Landore, Grandma was told startling news concerning the Estate which was so fresh in our minds after our visit to the heart of her family.

Some relations, not named Pryce, of her family had been revealed as having attempted to claim the Estate by engaging a barrister to read the documents they held.

"They have no right," Grandma said angrily. "As you've heard from the will of Elizabeth Seys Pryce, it goes to 'male heirs for ever' and they are not Pryces."

"But what right have you either?" put in my father, who was resigned to all this rigmarole he had heard so many times. "You are descended from the female line too."

"I don't want your opinion, John Matthews, thank you," and smiling triumphantly added "What do you think the barrister told these people?" She waited for the effect. "Just what I said. They haven't a hope as they are not of the male line."

"Neither are you Pryces," rubbed in my incorrigible father.

Ignoring this remark Grandma continued.

"We have had an offer from these people to pool all our documents together and engage a barrister to study them, there is to be a meeting in some hotel for this, but I don't think I'll go there. Some of you must though."

This was something I wouldn't miss for anything and Evelyn, Claudia and I went along that eventful summer evening to a hotel in Carmarthenshire. Perhaps the two branches of the family might join forces in making a successful claim and all would share in the Estate, which would solve everything.

As we walked up the road to the hotel I felt like a character in a drama, but this feeling left me as the only too familiar smell of beer and smoke hit us on entering the premises. The noisy chatter and clink of glasses accompanied us up the stairway to the room engaged for the meeting. Here, in spite of the polish on the furniture and the breeze from an open window, the penetrating smell of liquor from previous occupants lingered. Two rows of chairs had been arranged along walls facing each other. At the far end a table and chair stood against the third wall. Here, Uncle Isaac took his place while we filled the chairs along one wall. United as a family, we sat in battle formation, ready to face the enemy who had plotted to gain our inheritance.

I had never seen any of the men and women who now arrived and sat opposite us: such ordinary, decent-looking people. And these were the ones who had plotted to rob Willie Pryce of his rightful heritage! Perhaps I wanted them to look like the villains of a melodrama. Uncle Isaac wasted no time by saying:

"You have done a wicked thing in trying to claim the Estate without showing us. Why, your name isn't Pryce, and what does the will say? 'Male heirs for ever', that's what it says." By this time Uncle Isaac had lapsed into Welsh with which he was more articulate, and here his son took over as spokesman for the Pryce family.

He made a powerful speech, berating the enemy with the words 'We Pryces' at pertinent intervals, which so incensed them that he was challenged regarding the right he had to the Estate. At this, several began speaking at once, arguing with each other across the room.

Now a dagger was thrust into the very heart of our claim as a man, squaring his shoulders, flung at our spokesman, "What better right have you Pryces to the Boverton Estate than we have? Talk about the will. Why, she herself was a female wasn't she? And what right had she to will any part of the Estate to you?"

It was at this point that I began to doubt the validity of my grandmother's claim and my heart sank like lead as I recalled all the faith she had placed in it.

As the battle raged from side to side I heard nothing of it, except that it was words. I had been living in a romantic dream, nurtured constantly by Grandma.

The appearance of the landlord of the hotel told us that our time was up and we rose to leave, the spokesman of each side making a hurried arrangement for settling our differences.

Grandma listened with piteous eagerness to our account of the meeting, which she would have loved to have attended. I was glad she hadn't heard what I had. Let her go on dreaming and hoping, though I began to lose heart about it.

The result of this meeting was an arrangement for members of both sides to meet at a solicitor's office in Llanelli. It was exciting to realise that at last perhaps there was some hope. We each took along a pound towards the barrister's fee.

What a mixed group we made! Teachers, bank clerks, miners mainly, farmers, and of course William Pryce, who Grandma was convinced was the heir to the Estate. He was a miner too, delicate and pale and to me looked like a refined stage hero. The solicitor, whose father had also worked for the family, explained the position to us. We must understand that none of us except Willie had any claim and we were there to help him financially. However, he was sure that as this was the case, in the event of a successful result, Willie should have half of the Estate and the other half would be shared among those members who had contributed and were his near relatives. This sounded reasonable enough until Willie, with a typical heroic gesture, stood up and said that he would accept no more than the others and the Estate should be equally shared. Respectful glances flew towards where he had now taken his seat, where his slight form was lost in the burliness of a farmer nearby. I felt proud of him.

On the wall was fixed a huge family tree on which we had to write our names. All the documents we had brought were handed over and now all was in the hands of the barrister.

The day of the solicitor's meeting was a happy one for Grandma, who couldn't have enough of the details when we reached home. "What did I tell you, John? Now we shall have justice done."

"Don't you be so sure," was his reply.

And he was right to be so doubtful. There was at least one important document missing which was essential to any hope of success and the excitement died down as time went on. Grandma became very quiet whenever there was mention of the Estate. I think she was quietly breaking her heart.

Occasionally something would happen to revive my hopes: like the day we had a visit from a man who came from the village of Llanedi, where Grandma and her brother William had lived with their parents at a house called 'Plas Newydd'. He knew that Grandma was of the family and said he couldn't understand why we didn't fight for the Estate, as everyone in Llanedi knew that it should have gone to the Pryce family. Wearily my mother explained how we had tried and that we had no more money to risk.

"Borrow it. It's worth a fortune by now," he advised.

But nothing was done about it and I think Grandma was the only one in The Station Inn who still romantically dreamed of the Estate.

Soon after this I was sitting in a bus going from Gorseinon to Swansea, when I felt someone poking a bony finger in my back, I turned round, and there behind me sat a disreputable looking old woman. She looked like a gipsy.

"You belong to the Pryces of Capel Hendre, don't you?" she asked in a very loud voice. I felt embarrassed as everyone in the bus could hear. "Yes," I whispered.

"Then why don't you do something about the Estate?" she asked, or rather shouted. I was astounded. What did this dirty old woman have to do with it?

"All of you. Aye, I could tell you a lot, but there, it's up to you, isn't it?" and she was still speaking as she got off the bus at The Mile End Inn, near Swansea. I must find out who she could be.

When I asked my father if he knew anything about her he said he'd enquire, which he did. She was a Mrs. Turner nee Morris, who had had the reputation as a young girl of being exceptionally clean and was noted for making leather gloves for the men working at the Cwmfelin Steel and Tinplate Works, Swansea. I learned that she lived in a small cottage and it wasn't until I walked up the lane leading to the cottage that I realised what a hovel the old woman lived in. She was quite pleasant to me and we sat on chairs in the dark kitchen, lit by an oil lamp on the table. Her husband, red-faced and overweight in his navy blue flannel shirt sleeves, sprawled over the table and didn't utter a word. I confess I felt rather nervous, as she had been so aggressive on the bus. She didn't stop talking but I failed to make sense of what she was saying.

"See this desk?" she asked, pointing to a beautiful little bureau which was hidden in the shadows of the room, "This came from 'Plas Newydd'." This *did* surprise me and I wondered how she had come by this bit of furniture from Grandma's old home. It had been badly neglected but still showed quality.

"And I've got documents to prove."

"Prove what?" I asked.

"Never you mind, my girl. I'm keeping them till the day. And see here," pointing out places on a very soiled map above the bureau, "this is the property." Her dirty hands roamed over the map. She read out a list of farms, extending throughout Carmarthenshire and Glamorganshire. There was something very familiar about the names and I realised that I had heard Evelyn read them from Grandma's documents on Sunday nights.

I was no wiser leaving the cottage than when I went in, as she was so secretive. But how did this dirty old hag get hold of the bureau and the documents and the map? And possibly other things from 'Plas Newydd'. We couldn't even guess, unless she belonged somewhere in the family. We heard nothing more of her except that she became more and more slovenly and she and her husband ended their days in an old folks' home.

The final effort made by our family towards finding out where we stood regarding the Estate entailed a visit to the National Library of Wales, Aberystwyth.

I went with my Uncle Isaac, Uncle Lewis and Uncle Daniel by coach to Aberystwyth and up to the imposing Library. Here we were allowed to study the important documents giving the family tree of the Seyses. Although we sat in the same room as the assistant who gave them to us, we had to sign for them first. My uncles, probably unused to sitting quietly in libraries, fidgeted and one of them began to hum softly. This sounded terribly loud in the scholarly atmosphere and hard looks from other readers silenced him.

We were able to trace the Seys family from the early seventeenth century but when we arrived at the name of Grandma's ancestor, Elizabeth Seys Pryce, we were bitterly disapponted. We read that she had married her cousin Evan Seys of Boverton Castle. That was the end of our searching. There was no mention of her marriage to Lewis Pryce, and it is from one of their sons that our family is descended.

We came away defeated. I looked at the three old men and marvelled at their faith in what must be a lost cause. Grandma's faith and defiance continued throughout my young life. If it was a forlorn hope she handed down to me I cherished it, and loved her for its strength and, yes, beauty.

CHAPTER SIXTEEN

"So you want to go to the English chapel in Swansea, like Evelyn and Ray do you? Our Welsh chapel isn't good enough for you, I suppose." Grandma's sarcasm was cutting.

"It's not that, Grandma," and I tried to explain the attraction of attending the large, popular chapel in town, where I could understand all the sermons and where there were no verses to be learned and recited aloud before everyone at the Sunday School. The numbers in our chapel were dwindling depressingly, and anyway it was exciting to go to Swansea on a Sunday.

Coaxed by my mother, who pointed out that although the chapel in Swansea was English, it was still Baptist, Grandma allowed me to go, with Dick accompanying me.

One Sunday morning we had a visiting preacher, since our minister had volunteered as a padre in the army. As soon as I saw him ascend the pulpit I thought:

"Oh, No! He's exactly like Chester Conklin," (the film comic with cross eyes and a wobbly moustache) and I prayed silently that the same thought wouldn't strike Dick too, or we should both start giggling. I was thankful to observe that he had not observed the similarity though I felt that at any moment he would.

The sermon was over and halfway through the last prayer, in a dead silence between the preacher's words, Dick whispered "Isn't he like Chester Conklin!" It was a relief at last to remove the handkerchief I had stuffed into my mouth to stifle my giggles. I dared not let Grandma know all this.

My Landore friends all went to Welsh chapels, but there was a girl in my form in school whom I persuaded to come along to Sunday School with me. She lived in Swansea and we usually had tea at her home and attended the evening service from there. Eventually we were both baptised, thus becoming members, but before that I had a distressing experience.

I hadn't been told that this special Sunday was Temperance Sunday and a rousing sermon on the evils of strong drink was given. I sat enthralled and horrified as we were told of the homes destroyed by drunken fathers, and of starving children who waited in the freezing cold while their wicked parents sat inside public houses drinking their earnings away.

It was like watching a melodrama. The preacher's voice rose and rose in condemnation. I could visualise the wretchedness portrayed so emotionally, but as yet my mind hadn't conected it with my home. In full stride now the preacher demanded that all public houses be closed permanently and the evil wiped out at one stroke. The congregation was stirred and when he said "Please stand up all who would see the closure of all public houses," nearly the whole of the membership rose eagerly.

"Yes, he's quite right," I thought and stood up with them.

This was an experience that shook my soul. On my way home in the tram I sat thinking unhappily.

"I am living in a wicked home. My Grandma is supposed to be a good Christian and she is kept by the sale of strong drink. And so is Mama and Dada and all of us." I hated my family and myself for this hypocrisy. The walk up Station Road and under the railway bridge, which usually seemed so long, was over too soon. Slowly I walked up our street, my thoughts frantic and wretched. I stopped outside The Station Inn in the quiet of that Sunday evening. When at last I knocked at the door it was in misery and bewildered temper. To eat my supper would have choked me. When Grandma coaxed me I saw her as an alien,

"Oh, Grandma, how can you be like this?" I thought, my mind full of the condemning words I had heard a short time earlier.

"There's something the matter with Hannah fach. Find out what's happened, Cassie," but my mother could get nothing out of me.

"It's something to do with the English Chapel, I know. Evelyn, you were there tonight. What happened?"

"I didn't go. It's Temperance Sunday. One of the deacons warned me, so Gwennie and I went for a walk instead."

That explained everything and they were all very kind. Evelyn was told off for not warning me, a sensitive child.

It took a long time for me to accept that my family were not wicked, but the feeling of shame didn't leave me, although my mother reminded me that when she was a little girl the preachers used to put up at Kingsbridge Inn and they wouldn't stay there if they didn't respect Grandma, would they? Hadn't one of them remarked, "She ought to be in the pulpit, not the pub." This helped. It was a relief to learn that publicans in the bible didn't mean owners of public houses, but tax-gatherers.

It was some comfort, too, when Grandma whispered when she saw my worried little face, "Never mind, Hannah fach, you won't have to live at the inn when we have the Stat."

People who vowed never to touch strong drink used to 'Sign the Pledge' and were given a certificate on which they signed their names. This was invariably framed and hung up in one of the rooms at home. Even children were encouraged to sign and one of my young friends had an unpleasant experience over hers. One afternoon, when coming home from school, a woman stood in her doorway with a jug in her hand and asked if she would fetch a half pint of beer from the public house nearby. My friend didn't like to refuse, took the jug and the money and was given a halfpenny for carrying out the errand. She was late reaching home and when she told her mother the reason there was a frightful row.

"You naughty girl! Do you know what you've done? You've

broken your pledge by going into a public house and carrying a jug of beer in the street. You've broken your sacred pledge."

Racing upstairs the poor child fully expected to find her 'pledge' broken into pieces on the floor, with glass all over the place. But her certificate hung serene and safe on the wall. This 'pledge' business was difficult for a little girl to understand.

****

The evening I was baptised, along with twenty-four other members of the Sunday School, was a moving experience. We had had several talks with the minister so that we understood what we were doing. The water in the well below the pulpit of the chapel was heated and a cosy fire was lit in the adjoining lecture hall where our parents waited with towels and hot tea. I confess to a concern for the appearance of my hair after immersion, but as everyone came up the steps of the well with dripping hair, to be covered in large towels by our teachers, it did not matter that my hair would be straight. I wanted terribly to be good and when, soon after we had to write a compositon on what we wished to be when we were grown up I felt completely honest when I wrote 'a good woman'.

During this 'goody-goody' period I won first prize in the Sunday School Scripture Examination and was told I would be taken by our Superintendent to W.H. Smith's to choose my prize. I knew exactly what I wanted, a book of poems; Byron's if possible. But I found to my dismay he had bought one already. Not Byron, but "The Poems of Adam Lindsay Gordon', an Australian poet of whom I had never heard. I was very disapponted and as there was half a crown over after paying for it I was allowed to choose another book.

I bought 'The Rosery' over which I cried and cried; it was so beautiful. I tried to like my prize but the setting of the poems didn't appeal to me at all. Grandma was reconciled to the idea of my attending an English chapel and by now very proud that I'd done so well at the examination.

Although it was all right to go to the 'Pictures', the theatre was taboo. Even when my mother and father had given us permission to go we always asked Grandma's leave also. This was refused untill the day Evelyn and Ray wanted to see 'Charley's Aunt' at the Grand Theatre in Swansea. Pretending it was a kind of concert held in the Albert Hall, they asked Grandma if she would take them. This was the hall where Grandma liked to see 'Poole's Myriorama', a lantern slide lecture. She took me once and we saw performing horses on the screen, which delighted her. She loved horses. My mother told me that when Grandma's father had died, her mother re-married. Grandma had said, "I was only a little girl and everyone went to the wedding on horseback." How romantic, I thought, and I could picture my great-great-grandmother seated perhaps on her horse with Grandma held lovingly in front of her.

But to return to 'Charley's Aunt'. Trusting she wouldn't recognise the way they were going, Ray, Evelyn and Grandma set off for the Grand Theatre where they enjoyed the farce immensely, Grandma as much as anyone. As it was a Saturday matinee it was still daylight when they came out. They were half way up Oxford Street, which was crowded with people, when Grandma stopped.

"What's the name of that place we've just been in? It wasn't the Albert Hall, was it?" The girls didn't know what to say, and people were staring.

"Answer me, drat you!"

"It was the Grand Theatre."

In silence they got into a tram and no one spoke all the way home. The word 'theatre' wasn't mentioned for a long time.

When a good play came along they simply had to ask her permission, relying on her keen sense of humour to allow them to go, but it was a struggle.

"What! Let you go to the Grand Theatre indeed. Certainly not! Howyr bach!" (Goodness gracious), she said with sarcasm. "I've never been in such a wicked place."

"Now, Grandma, what about 'Charley's Aunt'?"

"Well, yes. It was very funny. Remember that part where" and as she reminisced about it they would refresh her memory eagerly, knowing she would have to relent in the end.

****

To Grandma, dancing was another 'sin' though the girls were able to attend the dancing classes held in Swansea without her knowing, it was when the annual balls came round that the tussle for permission started. There were the evening dresses to be made by my mother, tactfully cut out in the clubroom to avoid the disapproval in Grandma's eyes. 'Balchder' (vanity) was another sin. Weldon's Ladies Fashion Books were studied, patterns bought and the clubroom's long table was splendid for cutting. I spent hours crayoning the pretty dresses in Weldon's and when a fancy dress ball was held I enjoyed helping Ray and Evelyn to dress their long hair accordingly.

When Evelyn went as a Grecian Lady, her gown of white muslin had gold braid in a Grecian key design round the hem and neck. What braid was over I draped through her piled-up hair, as in the fashion book. Ray went as a gipsy, which suited her dark eyes and hair. She wore a red skirt, fullsleeved white blouse with a black velvet corset affair, laced across the front.

All preparations had to be very secret until the great night and the girls were dressed. Before he went to the war they were usually escorted by our handsome young cousin, Glyn Daniel, who was a good dancer.

"What do you want a taxi for? The neighbours will think we are made of money," Grandma complained and the girls always left looking miserable, though no doubt they cheered up as soon as they were out of sight of Station Inn.

My father would slip downstairs when he heard the taxi bringing them home, and make some hot cocoa for them. In the morning I would hear all about their glorious evening.

****

Our school held a concert in which my form did a 'historical tableau' item, and I was Boadicea, Queen of the Iceni. For this my mother gave me Evelyn's Grecian dress, adapted to fit me, though a Grecian gown for a British queen was not very sensible, but the crown I wore perhaps redeemed that fault.

One of my friends represented Queen Elizabeth the First. She was tall and regal-looking until someone accidentally pushed her crown lop-sided and she looked drunk, quite spoiling the group photograph of the tableau our form portrayed.

Evelyn and I now shared a bed in the front bedroom. She was a good church worker, in the Life Brigade and the sewing class. Every morning before going downstairs to breakfast she opened her New Testament and read the passage for the day as given in the booklet of bible readings. Reluctantly I felt I ought to do so too and sometimes evaded this by just closing my testament when she was looking, so that she would think I had been reading it.

Although only five years my senior, Evelyn was more sedate and took life much more seriously. Her hair was drawn back severely while I loved to have wavy or curly hair. This she considered rather common and any efforts at glamorising myself were discouraged.

"Wipe that stuff off your face. Your sister wouldn't dream of using such rubbish," rebuked my mother.

Dick and I were friends, but he was interested in football and I wished he'd been older so that he could escort me to dances as other girls' brothers did.

CHAPTER SEVENTEEN

"This summer you shall come to Llandrindod Wells with the girls and me."

I kissed and hugged Grandma at this wonderful news. Dick was too young to come with us, but Ray, Gwen, Evelyn and I went by train from Swansea. It was a long, exciting journey. The train stopped at every small station and we dashed from window to window of our compartment to see if the cows in the fields were standing up, which meant fine weather. There were cries of disappointment when we spotted some lying down.

On reaching Llandrindod there was a 'scene' when Grandma found one suitcase had been left on the platform in Swansea and it had to be sent on later. We stayed at a boarding house and every morning the girls accompanied Grandma to the shops to buy food which the landlady cooked. Sometimes Grandma helped her by shelling the peas. We had brought butter from Swansea market as Grandma thought we couldn't possibly get such good butter anywhere else. On the day we ran out of butter, the girls were told to send a telegram to my father asking him to send more butter on the train, which we would meet the next day. Evelyn and Ray, being young ladies by now didn't like the idea of going into the post office and writing a telegram saying, 'Please send three pounds of butter', so after some discussion this was how they worded it, 'Adornment for the staff of life urgently needed by morning train'. They decided not to tell Grandma about this and the butter arrived. She wondered why my father had sent four pounds though.

At last I could see the pierrots in chalk-white baggy trousers and jackets with big black bobbles. Their faces were ghostly white, too, like circus clowns, and they wore hats with black bobbles.

But this wasn't Grandma's idea of enjoyment. She said "Put your coats and hats on, girls as it's a place of worship we're going to and it gets cold in the tent in the evenings." And all five of us would set forth for the revival meeting at which the famous Welsh preacher, Evan Roberts, held hundreds enthralled by his stirring sermons. But the girls were bored to tears and longed, as to be honest I did, to escape. When they saw that Grandma was too engrossed to notice they crept out and hurried off to one of the evening shows. Grandma wanted explanations of course, but it was easy to get lost in the crowd and she had to accept that they were somewhere in the marquee all the time. At least she appeared to accept their explanation. Perhaps she realised that young girls needed more than spiritual uplift when on summer holidays.

Although they were allowed to stroll around Llandrindod on their own while Grandma took the waters, I wasn't so lucky and had to accompany her. There I had to sit while she downed her half-pint of sulphur or saline in that evil-smelling Pump Room where the waters were drawn from pumps very much like those for beer at The Station Inn. Then followed our walk to the chalybeate spring: here water dripped from a gap in the grassy bank in the park. We had to line up, Grandma holding the small medicine glass in one hand and gripping my reluctant hand in the other. Slowly we trudged through the unavoidable puddles as our turn drew nearer and nearer, until we had reached the spot where she held the glass under the drips. It took ages for the horrid stuff to fill the glass to the brim.

"Now, drink up, Hannah fach. Every drop mind. Its full of iron and will make you strong." The idea of being filled with iron disgusted me and the chalybeate water tasted like licking rusty nails, salt and ink.

Llandrindod Wells was very fashionable for holidays at that time and in the evenings we walked past the grand hotels where the guests were having dinner. We admired the beautiful gowns of the ladies and envied them for being able to afford such fine places. In the mornings there were bowls matches. Competitors came from as far away as London to try their skill and win silver cups.

One morning in the Pump Room Grandma got into conversation with another water-drinker who, when she was told we came from Landore, said she had never heard of it and what a pretty name it was. That Landore could be described as anything but ugly and smoky was very unlikely; but much beloved, yes certainly. The industrial part of Swansea, where every metal was worked, was nostalgically lovely perhaps in the eyes of many workers who went off to America to find work. It was so easy to escape from Landore to the lovely sandy bays around Swansea that a halo of beauty over the whole town painted itself in the inhabitants' eyes and memories.

At Llandrindod Grandma would rest in the afternoon. I had made a friend of our landlady's daughter and she came back with us to spend a holiday in Landore. One afternoon in Llandrindod she took me to her aunt's to tea and when she told me there was a piano there, I was delighted. There wasn't one at her house. It was a long walk through the country lanes to the cottage where we found her aunt busily laying tea for us and her uncle already seated at the table. I was soon seated at the piano playing away, and no doubt showing off, as Agnes couldn't play at all.

During the meal the uncle asked if my family was musical and I said my father's family were, but I'd never heard my mother sing a note, or Grandma Daniel either. But my father's sisters were all good singers and one could play the piano beautifully. "In fact," I said, "you could say music runs in the family like wooden legs." There was a silence which I took to be disgust at my showing off so much. On the way back to the boarding house I learned that Agnes's uncle had a wooden leg. I felt dreadful.

One highlight of that first Llandrindod holiday was an afternoon at the pierrot show. I was wearing my best Leghorn straw hat, trimmed with a huge scarlet poppy in front. The lady singer must have fancied it, as she asked me after the show if she might borrow it to wear for the evening performance. I was thrilled at this honour: stage people had such glamour for me and there we sat in the front row, Agnes and me, for nothing, and I longed to stand up and tell the audience "That's MY best hat she's wearing;" but of course I just watched and felt a new respect for my hat.

Agnes and I were out shopping for her mother one day when she met a friend and they started talking in some strange language and I couldn't understand a word. Agnes told me it was Swiss, which I accepted and thought they were very clever as I could never speak French so rapidly. Agnes laughed and explained that it wasn't Swiss at all but 'back-slang', which she promised to teach me. This she did and I didn't mind going home a bit as she was coming back with us, and I was dying to teach Eira this new secret way of talking. It has been very useful in company and is so even to this day when we telephone and have something very private to say. It was simple enough, really. You had to take each syllable and insert 'AIG' in the middle, so that a word like 'TAKE' became 'TAIGAKE', but a word beginning with a vowel, such as 'AS' became 'AIGAS'. Eira mastered it quickly, so did Dick, but Evelyn didn't bother, saying it was rubbish. Grandma would become furious when she heard Dick and me planning some escapade, like going to the Fair; our back-slang running along fluently but utterly unintelligibly to her ears. My father learned to say one phrase only. 'SHAIGUT AIGUP' which you will have translated as 'SHUT UP'.

****

During term-time Friday night was Mackworth Night for Dick and his friends and for me and mine. We didn't have to worry about train fares as the school provided us with season tickets and there was a convenient train from Landore to High Street Station which was quite near the Mackworth Hotel in Swansea. The hotel meant nothing to us: we were making for the Mackworth Restaurant adjoining it. But first, on entering the cafe, we stopped at the counter on the right where chocolates were made. Here we bought our weekend supply. Here, too we watched the white-hatted chef mix cakes and toss pancakes before our very eyes. Clutching our bags of chocolates we ignored the marble-topped tables and high, glass-fronted cupboards in one wall where you could put sixpence in a slot and take out a sandwich or pasty and a cup of tea, to eat at a table. This wasn't good enough for us. We'd pass through the glass doors into the restaurant where waitresses served at white linen topped tables. Not these either for us! We were glared at by them as if to say, 'Here come those nuisances of schoolchildren. No hope of a tip from them,' as we marched right down to the far end.

Here, facing the stage with its red velvet curtain were several rows of long seats, just like church pews, with shelves for our coffee-dashes and chips. We tried to get into the front row, especially the boys who liked the charming young singer, Laurie Melville, grand-daughter of a famous Swansea actor. A young lad in topper and tails did tap-dancing and sang sophisticated love-songs, and a powerful soprano sang 'When you wore a tulip, a sweet yellow tulip, and I wore a red, red rose'. Some of the more boisterous boys waited until she reached the word 'yellow' and then shouted 'Yell' at the top of their voices. There were sketches in which the whole cast took part. These were often repeated so that we knew the words as they were spoken. It was a grand show and well worth the price of our meal; ninepence.

One Friday evening my friend Gwyneth and I arrived too late for a pew seat and we had to sit at one of the tables to be served by a waitress. For some reason Gwyneth decided to do some homework because the waitress kept us waiting a long time. Just when the food arrived, the bottle of ink tipped all over the chalk-white table cloth and we had to eat up and get out. Why Gwyneth had to do homework on Friday when there was Saturday ahead I couldn't understand. She was going somewhere special on Saturday it seemed. Anyway, we were determined to be in a pew seat in good time in future.

****

The long-promised return from Africa of my cousin Trevor, who had become the hero of my thoughts, came at last. This was the first time for me to meet him. It was the first time, too, for him to meet his half-sisters, Gwen and Ray.

Trevor, a former Royal Navy Commander, had gone to Africa as a planter and also became a sportsman and 'white hunter'. He organised safaris for the rich men who could afford such pleasures. I listened enthralled to his talk of engaging camp boys, chop boys and beaters when preparing a safari. When all was safely arranged and the quarry sighted, Trevor told his employers it was time to shoot, and theirs was all the glory of the kill. I thought it unfair that he did all the spadework but realised that he was only doing the job he was hired to do.

I followed eagerly his accounts of elephant hunts and of

suddenly coming across lions and rhinoceroses and I made him promise to write to me often when he got back. I tried to visualise the scene he described when he called at a village and found many of its inhabitants had been eaten by a crocodile: how he had tethered a goat as bait by the river's edge. For nights Trevor lay hidden nearby, his gun at the ready. I felt proud when I heard that he had shot the creature and how grateful the poor natives had been. He brought home an elephant's tusk and a rhinoceros's horn for Claudia, who displayed them on her parlour mantelpiece.

Trevor took us to the Grand Theatre in Swansea. We sat in a box. This disappointed me as we could see into the wings. This revealed the ordinariness of the back-stage, taking away much of the glamour. The girls on the stage ogled Trevor boldly, and no wonder! He was so handsome, tall and fair, with bright blue eyes.

After his first few days he impressed us all by saying that he was 'popping' up to Scotland to play golf with a charming girl he had met on the ship coming home from Africa. "Just for the weekend, Grandma. And Uncle Jack, you'll cash a cheque for me, will you?" Oh, it was very elegant, even grand to be able to talk of 'popping' up to Scotland: all that way for one weekend and just to play golf!

Life was very tame after Trevor left, but his letters came as he had promised. They were amusing, sometimes terrifying and often in verse. He sent Claudia a bracelet made from the hair from an elephant's tail. This looked like a bangle of stiff black liquorice with a gold clasp and was supposed to be a lucky charm, though it couldn't be called an attractive piece of jewellery by any means. It was a link between Claudia and her only brother.

While he was with us he went to see his old Nanny, who was delighted that he remembered her, and she still thought of him as 'Boysie'. When Grandma warned him about his dangerous way of living, he laughed and said, "Don't worry about me, Grandma. I shall die with my boots on and my gun in my hand." But this was not to be. Several years later he was taken ill, rushed to hospital in Salisbury, Southern Rhodesia, operated on and died.

I shall never forget the look on Claudia's face when she heard the news. She was utterly stricken. To have seen so little of him during the whole of their lives, having been brought up in different homes and meeting so briefly and having had such a happy time on his last visit; for this tragedy to happen just when she half-expected him home again and had only recently bought a new carpet and easy chair for his bedroom!

Trevor had sent me a long necklace of a hundred ivory beads. They were graded from tiny ones to one large round one and were heavy to wear, but I valued them as they were made from the ivory of elephants he had shot. His men had carved each bead and he had polished them and had them made into a necklace for me.

So Claudia had her bangle and I the beads to keep fresh our memories of Trevor.

WHITE HUNTER (To my Cousin Trevor)

He saw great beauty in a pride
of lions, sunning in calm serenity.
He who had led
adventurous safaris often said,
"I live with my gun at the ready,
my life in my hands. I shall die
with my boots on." He carved ivory
beads from elephant tusks for me;
spent lonely nights by croc-infested banks
to lure and kill these man-eaters, that poor
black natives should not suffer more
of human loss. From them he craved no thanks.

. . . .

Yet, in a clinic bed, his boots aside,
his rifle safely stacked away,
stricken with sudden illness, quiet he lay,
and in merciful unconsciousness, he died.

CHAPTER EIGHTEEN

The term dragged along, but there was plenty to do during the lunch hour, apart from roaming round Woolworth's and sitting in the reading room in the Library.

One day, Gwyneth and I joined a crowd of girls drawn to the window of a chemist's shop. It showed the picture of a beautiful young lady applying Icilma face cream with graceful gestures to her peach-like cheeks: her eyes were closed with bliss. It was the first face cream we had ever seen.

Some one in the crowd read the advertisement aloud, pronouncing the word as 'Ickle-ma', which amused us so that we always called it 'Ickle-ma' after that. Of course we bought a jar each and that evening used half of it, expecting the magic results to show immediately.

"What's that scent you're wearing, Doris?"

I knew that Grandma was cross with me when she called me Doris instead of Hannah fach.

"Icilma,"I replied, despairingly, knowing that I dared not use it again at home. But hopefully I explained "It's not scent really. It's face cream. It makes your skin soft and lovely."

"You don't need it," she retorted, and muttering 'balchder, balchder' (vanity, vanity) Grandma marched out of the kitchen.

****

Grandma must have been aware of how weary she was becoming, because she decided to retire from the 'business' and went to live with Claudia and her children a few doors away from the back entrance of the Station Inn.

My father and Gwen went to Cardiff to see how little Olive was getting along, which resulted in their bringing her back with them, to live with Claudia. Grandma liked to come in to the inn for an hour in the evening as long as there was something for her to do. She finished the darning my mother had found for her to do, looked round restlessly, then just slipped away to her new home. It happened time and time again. This resulted in a general hunt for socks and stockings that needed mending, and even some that did not, simply to keep her with us. Dick and I missed seeing her sitting on the settle, faintly interested in our homework and keeping an eye on the clock. If one of the girls was still out of doors at ten o'clock she became anxious, then angry. Young people must be kept under proper control, she maintained, and my mother told Evelyn, Ray and Gwen that they were lucky to be allowed to attend these rare dances, arriving home later then ten o'clock.

"When your father and I were courting," my mother said, looking towards Evelyn, "we used to go to the Grand Theatre in

Swansea to the opera, but I had to pretend it was a concert at the Albert Hall and I was on pins during the second act, as I had to catch a tram so as to be home by the time Grandma insisted was right."

The girls listened with sympathy as my mother continued, "So, as soon as the second act ended we had to rush for the tram, then up to The Station Inn and your father was sometimes lucky enough to catch a tram back to town in time for him to see the last act."

****

The darning was in a neat pile and Grandma remained sitting, her hands clasped together on her lap, her tired eyes straying to the papers scattered on the table, all part of our homework.

Dick grabbed a ruler and neatly drew a firm line in red ink under a finished sum. In doing so, one of my papers was knocked to the floor and Grandma, curious, picked it up.

My heart nearly stopped as it was a code-letter I had painstakingly worked out to be given to the boy I imagined I was in love with. I prayed she wouldn't read it.

"What's all this then?"

Grandma peered through her spectacles at the mysterious hieroglyphics and Dick looked up, suddenly interested.

I snatched the paper up before his inquisitive eyes could see my precious love letter.

"It's only a bit of algebra, Grandma," I lied quickly. This she accepted as she had no idea what algebra looked like, or that it was connected with maths.

"I've told you Grandma," I hurried to explain, "We don't call it sums in school, we call it mathematics," at which she smiled.

"So Doris Matthews is doing Matthewmatics, is she?"

"Isn't Grandma clever, Dick. Did you hear what she said about mathematics?" I gabbled, hastening to fold away the paper and hide it deep among the books in my school satchel.

****

Grandma's plan for Ray to attend Training College to become a teacher was shattered the evening Ray disappeared. My cousin had gone out and was expected home by ten o'clock, but there was no sign of her. Her sister Gwen was silent and when the fateful telegram arrived saying that Ray had got married, Grandma suspected that Gwen knew about the elopement.

The atmosphere in the kitchen was like that at a funeral. Grandma sat silent, but furious. To marry at seventeen and to an Englishman Grandma hadn't even met, as Ray hadn't dared to bring him to the inn to be interrogated by Grandma as to his religious beliefs, was dreadful in her eyes.

My father was very hurt as he had expected that one day, when Ray would be in her twenties, she would ask him to give her away and in a chapel wedding, of course.

A few days later an apologetic letter from the runaways came, assuring Grandma that she was very, very happy.

"Who gave her away then?" she demanded of Gwen.

"Glyn Daniel," Gwen readily replied, Glyn being a cousin on Grandpa Daniel's side. It was he who had always escorted the girls to the elegant annual balls in Swansea.

"Him?" Grandma snorted. "That's what comes of gallivanting about and dancing with all sorts." But it gave her no comfort to be assured that these balls were very decorous occasions about which I had heard on the day following. How I had envied them and longed to be old enough to attend such exciting events - but Dick was too young to accompany me and much preferred playing football.

I could imagine the girls entering the ball-room, each being given a programme and the eager rush of young gentlemen to sign their names besides the dances, as partners. I loved to read these cherished, dainty programmes which lay alongside the booklets of 'papier poudre' used for freshening up between dances, in the dressing table drawer in their bedroom. How could Grandma say they 'danced with all sorts' when the men wore evening suits and white gloves so as to avoid soiling the beautiful evening gowns with perspiring hands? 'Dancing with all sorts' indeed! I fumed at her words.

Feelings simmered down after a while, but I missed Ray's help with my homework and I caught Grandma looking sadly at Aunty Sally's photograph now and again. She was probably thinking about Ray and wondering if she was really happy in her new life, far away in the north of England somewhere.

****

Grandma's retirement meant less and less talk of the Estate. She spent Sunday evenings at home with Claudia and her two children so there were no more 'document sessions'.

Knowing that as soon as summer was coming Grandma would plan the annual holiday at Llandrindod Wells my mother had to write to the landlady of the boarding house where, year after year, Grandma stayed. I overheard my parents talking about this.

"Doctor Thomas told me that she mustn't on any account go to Llandrindod Wells this summer; it's too high up," said my mother.

"Well, Cassie, I don't fancy having to break *that* bit of news to her, that's all," my father replied.

Sure enough, Grandma was full of plans for her fortnight at "The Wells" as she called her favourite spa, and when told of the doctor's advice she was furious.

"Of course I'm going to Llandrindod. I always do, don't I? And why not, I'd like to know," she snorted. Patiently my mother explained that it was too high in the hills for her health.

"Where am I expected to go then? I'm not going to the seaside. We've got plenty of that in Swansea," she argued stubbornly.

It was a relief when Doctor Thomas suggested that as she was set on going to the country it would be all right for her to go to Builth Wells with Claudia. But no children! There she could still take the waters in which she had such faith. But she didn't enjoy Builth Wells nearly as much as her familiar, beloved Llandrindod Wells.

****

During that long summer holiday I went with my father's two sisters to St. Athan in the Vale of Glamorgan for a week. Uncle J.W's brother was taking a batch of the schoolboys in his form to work on the harvest in the farms.

The boys were put up at the local Grammar School while we stayed at the only available lodgings, the Police Station. St. Athan's was a quiet, pretty village, only a few miles from the coast, so my younger aunt and I were able to bathe in the sea. While chatting to the constable's wife I learned that we were not far from Llantwit Major, which I knew from Grandma's documents was the area where Boverton Castle stood. The Estate sprang once again to my mind.

Here, perhaps, was a chance to visit the much-discussed castle at last. I asked her if it was possible to walk to Llantwit Major and she said it would be a long walk and since it was a beautiful day "Why not take a picnic lunch and spend the day there?" So we set off on our long walk along leafy lanes towards Llantwit Major, hoping to see the castle where my ancestors had lived. My mind pictured the place on which Grandma and her family centred their hopes.

"Any minute now, as we turn a corner, I shall see it," I thought, "like the lovely castles I've read about; grand and stately surely." Elizabeth Seys Pryce had died there. Where was she buried I wondered; might I even see her grave? At last, we did turn a corner and it appeared to us across fields to our left; no stately home, just an ivy-covered ruin, half hidden by trees. I ought to have expected this, but it was a shock. We tramped, my aunt and I through high grass and weeds and were about to enter a stone doorway when a man and his dog appeared. He stopped us and said that the land belonged to a farmer, so we were trespassing and would we please leave.

As we walked back to the road I wondered what he would say if I'd told him all about Grandma and her family and what they felt about the castle and its estate. My aunt made no remark. I didn't expect her to. She wasn't interested. It wasn't *her* family that was connected with the place. It was her sister-in-law Cassie's mother and relations who talked about some Estate or other they were trying to claim. I pitied her for not having my romantic history.

Eventually we reached Llantwit Major where we paddled on the rocky beach. The sun had gone in and it was too cold to bathe; or perhaps I was cold from disillusionment.

On my return to Landore the first thing I asked my mother was if Grandma knew where I had been on holiday. What a relief it was to hear that all she had been told was that I had been away with my aunts somewhere.

The winter dragged on and a spurt of spring cleaning took over Claudia's household: Grandma as busy as anyone. Climbing on a chair to adjust a picture on a wall, she fell, and when I came home from school I heard she had fractured her leg. She was not a good patient being irritable at her inactivity. Day by day we saw her condition grow worse. Her muttering was quite unintelligible and the way her hands plucked continually was, to Claudia's nurse-trained mind, a bad sign.

Her eyes were fixed somewhere high above my head as I sought to understand what she wanted to tell me. Was she beyond thinking about the Estate in the unutterable weariness of her eight-three years? I wasn't to know. She died from pneumonia three days later.

I walked slowly home, feeling I had deserted the beloved figure lying in Claudia's front bedroom. There was no cosiness in the kitchen where Grandma had sat with me, ever fussing over my anaemia and where, on the supper table, the faded documents had been so often laid out for Evelyn to read aloud, so that their contents were impressed on our minds. There was nowhere in the inn where I could escape from the ache of her absence. I felt as if an old, well worn shawl had been roughly snatched from my thin shoulders, leaving an unbearable chill.

Aware only of my own misery, I ignored the suffering my mother had to endure in the well-meant condolences of friends, which she had to meet with a show of warmth and gratitude, especially when, against the family's wish for a private funeral, customers implored her to grant a public funeral, which meant an endless procession of men and women.

My mood of self pity was changed to anger the following day. We were sitting in Claudia's kitchen and I went to answer a knock on the front door. Two young girls stood outside.

"Could we please see Mrs. Daniel?"

"See Grandma?" I thought bankly. Hadn't they heard that she had died? "But my Grandmother is dead," I gulped.

"Oh, yes. We heard. That's why we'd like to see her," was their callous explanation.

"Certainly not. Go away," I said and, fuming, returned to the kitchen.

"It doesn't matter," said Claudia. "People do that sort of thing, you know. They like to have a last look at the person they knew. It's a kind thought, really."

"But it's dreadful and cruel," I argued. Then I recalled the day when Eira and I had called at Mrs. Hughes's up the street to see Dolly, the pretty little girl who had died. And I could almost feel again the chill of her icy, doll-like fingers which we touched so that we wouldn't have frightening dreams about her. Perhaps grown-ups held an idea of this sort, too, and my anger gave way to sadness as I left Claudia's house.

My mother was much too busy to make our 'mourning dresses' so a dressmaker came to measure us. The calf-length black silk dresses trimmed with narrow black lace were hideous and we looked like a group of crows as we sat in Claudia's parlour listening to the service. The ministers, and there were several, spoke feelingly of the respect in which Grandma was held. All the time I was saying to myself, "I'm not going to the funeral, I can't, I can't."

When the moment came for me to follow Evelyn into the cab I said I felt sick and ran to the toilet at the end of the back garden. I would stay here until they had gone. I stuffed my handkerchief into my mouth to stop crying aloud. I didn't feel at all sick, just utterly lost, for gone was the anchor of my dreams.

Seys Family Shield

THE SAMPLER

Among the attic's junk a rag I find,
crumpled and soiled into the rubbish flung:
now I remove, with shuddering touch, but kind,
the sampler Grandma worked when very young.
A cottage vaguely seen, its stitches frayed,
the wool in drabbest grey, the colours blurred:
her name in full, embroidered, 'wrought' it said
when she was eight years old, then her address. Memory stirred
through childhood days when I had gazed with awe
at this same sampler, framed above her bed,
its colours bright, the linen new. I saw
her as a child, my Grandma, long since dead.
I'll clean it, hang it on my bedroom wall:
we'll feel her love outpouring to us all.

While Grandma was alive I hadn't thought seriously about what I wanted to do with my life, but progressing through school led to the big decision regarding Training College or University. There was only one girl in my form, besides me, who wished to go to London. She was Enid, the one who had told me she was descended from Iolo Morgannwg, the Welsh poet. We went to London together and became fast friends.

The Principal of our Training College was a godly man who told us he was acting as our father while we were in London. At half-term, girls who lived too far to travel home were allowed to stay with friends or relations, provided a letter was produced from their parents giving permission.

I stayed with relations in London while Enid spent weekends at her uncle's home in Chelsea, for which he was Liberal Member of Parliament. The day he brought her back to college he was entertained to lunch at the Principal's house and later Enid introduced me to him. I learned that he was Aneurin Williams, father of Iolo Williams the poet and my mind flew back to the day my father had read that Iolo Morgannwg (Iolo of Glamorgan) had lived at Boverton Castle. All the excitement of the Estate was revived, as his name too was Iolo Williams. But this excitement soon died away as Grandma was dead and only I cared any longer.

The last echo of the Estate came during my final teaching practice. The library was silent as I climbed the ladder to the top shelf where the book I needed, 'The History of Syria' lay. While searching for it I saw a 'History of Wales'. Homesick, I brought it down along with 'The History of Syria' and began turning the pages. I knew where to look, the twelfth, thirteenth and seventeenth centuries. 'The History of Syria' must wait. I read that Boverton Castle was one of the homes of the earls of Gloucester and that, as far back as King John's reign it was where his divorced wife retired to. She was Isabel of Gloucester. It was to her that he had fled from the wrath of the barons.

I read on.

"Roger Seys was Attorney General for all Wales and Elizabeth his wife, Maid of Honour to Queen Elizabeth the First."

I grew so excited that the girl sitting next to me at the table asked me what was the matter.

"Look, Millie," I said, "read that paragraph." She did so.

"Well, what about it?" she asked.

"Seys is the name of my ancestors and they lived in Boverton Castle," I whispered.

Millie gave me a suspicious look, then said, "You rotten liar."

I didn't care. Never mind 'The History of Syria'. I wrote a long letter home quoting from the book. In my mother's reply she said "A pity Grandma isn't alive to read that. She would have been so proud."

POSTSCRIPT

I have visited Boverton Castle several times and wandered through the creeper-covered ruins. In the shadow of the castle stands Rock Cottage where the Hopkins family have lived for generations and know of the connection between the castle and the Pryce family.

In the back garden of Rock Cottage there is a recently walled-up tunnel entrance that led to the stables of the castle where at one time as many as sixty horses were housed.

Mrs. Hopkins told me that an eminent archaeologist has visited the ruins and a book on its history was lent to me. The only other copy lies in Cardiff Museum.

When I returned the book which Mrs. Hopkins cherishes, I was told that someone (not the farmer who works the surrounding land) had bought the castle ruin for a few hundred pounds.

THE VOSSES, SEYSES AND PRYCES OF BOVERTON PLACE

Boverton Place, commonly known as Boverton Castle, along with its extensive estates, belonged to the Voss family long before the Norman conquest. It appears that, like most other landed Welsh families, they were dispossessed by the Normans, but Boverton was restored to the Vosses later, as an act of gratitude for medical care rendered by a Gruffydd Voss to an incapacitated English baron.

Boverton was inherited by Gruffydd Voss's daughter Elizabeth, a Maid of Honour to Queen Elizabeth I.

She married Roger Seys, Attorney General of Wales.

In the early 1730's a female of the Voss-Seys line was mistress of Boverton Castle, namely Elizabeth Seys, daughter of Richard Seys, whose male heirs died without issue. Her father left the Estate to a cousin, Evan Seys, (on the principle of 'male heirs for ever').

Elizabeth Seys married this cousin who soon died without issue. She then married Lewis Price of Erwastad, Llanedi, continuing to live at Boverton Castle. By him she had seven children.

In succeeding generations the spelling of the family name was changed from 'Price' to 'Pryce'.

After the death of Lewis Price, she married twice but had no children by her later husbands.

Document No: D/D F431
Lease of Customary Land in Llantwit Major,
13th December 1661

This indenture made the 13th day of December in the second year of the Raigne of our Soveraigne Lord Charles by the grace of God, Kyng of England, Scotland, Fraunce and Ireland defender of the faith etcetera. Between Richard Seys of Bovertowne in the Countey of Glamorgan Esquier of the one part and Robert Walter of Battleys in the said Countey gentlemen of the other parts, Whereas........

The above is part of a document shown recently in Swansea Central Library. It lay among other old papers, of historic interest, faded and yellow. They were loaned by the Central Library, Cardiff, "for a period."